the truth about trusts

[a trustee's survival guide]

JACK W. EVERETT, CFP, AIMC

FTPC Publishing ■ California

FTPC Publishing
2140 Professional Drive, Suite 105
Roseville, CA 95661

e-mail: jeverett@quiknet.com
(916) 791-1447 ■ fax (916) 791-3444

Book design & copy editing by Sara Patton
Printed in the United States

Publisher's Cataloging-in-Publication
(Provided by Quality Books, Inc.)

Everett, Jack W.
     The truth about trusts : a trustee's survival guide /
Jack W. Everett.
     p. cm.
     Includes index.
     LCCN: 98-94845
     ISBN: 0-9626341-4-X

     1. Trusts and trustees — United States. 2. Living
trusts — United States — Popular works. 1. Title.

                                        QBI98-1772

Dedication

■ ■ ■ ■ ■ ■ ■ ■ ■ ■

To the memory of the two people who instilled the values that have guided my life — my parents Jack and Claire Everett. They both suffered from the effects of Alzheimer's Disease. My dad was inflicted with this long-term lingering disease and my mother exhausted herself with her loving care for him. A portion of the sales price of each book is being donated to the Sacramento Chapter of the Alzheimer's Association in their memory.

Contents

■ ■ ■ ■ ■ ■ ■

Acknowledgments

■ ■ ■ ■ ■ ■ ■ ■ ■ ■ ■ ■ ■ ■ ■

The Truth About Trusts would not have been possible without the help of a great many friends. They provided the necessary technical expertise, support, guidance, and encouragement needed to complete this challenge. I am grateful to all of them.

I am truly indebted to everyone who took the time to read the original manuscript and provide new insights and improvements, adding to the accuracy and readability of the text. Attorneys Charles A. ("Cap") Pinney, Michael Anderson, David Kelly, and David Erickson kept me on the straight and narrow. Fellow financial professionals Paul Pennington, CFP; David Haddock, CFP; Tom Frey, Ph.D., CFP; Lewis Potter, CLU, LUTCF; Jeff Davis, CFP; Jim Wendling, CFP; Joe Sullivan, CPA; Paul Richard, Executive Vice President of the National Center for Financial Education; and Jeffrey Lauterbach, President of American Guarantee and Trust, were all very generous with their time and practical improvements. A special thanks to my friend Al Capovilla who added the English professor's touch.

My design team was nothing short of spectacular. Kathi Dunn of Dunn+Associates captured the spirit of the book with her cover. Sara Patton took my "perfect" manuscript and made more improvements than I ever thought possible with her editing and layout skills. Susan Kendrick was the magician who transformed my rambling ideas into the back cover text.

It is very difficult to find humor to lighten up a topic as serious as trusts. I am thankful that a few cartoonists had the insights to do this. I am especially grateful to Bob Thaves (Frank & Ernest); Mell Lazarus (Momma) and John Rose (Financial Planning Publications, Inc.) for being gracious enough to allow me to include their work in this book.

I am also grateful for the encouragement and insights into publishing given to me by Dan Poynter, Mark Victor Hansen, Jennifer Sander, and Dottie Walters.

No thank you's would be complete without including my staff at the Financial and Tax Planning Center. Not only did they struggle to convert my scratchings to the printed word, but they offered a lot of encouragement. They tolerated my "writing days" away from the office and kept my financial planning practice running smoothly. Thank you Sally Erickson and Cynthia Adkins.

A special thanks to my wife Pat. She not only did some of the typing and tolerated my efforts at the office, she also tolerated all the time I took at home on this project. Throughout it all she still managed to support, encourage, and love me.

Thank you, everyone who played a part in producing *The Truth About Trusts*.

Introduction

■ ■ ■ ■ ■ ■ ■ ■ ■ ■ ■ ■ ■

Trusts have become a very popular estate planning tool over the last decade. When used properly, they can provide a relatively simple method of managing and transferring your assets with as little interference as possible from the Internal Revenue Service, the courts, and disgruntled heirs. They can also save your heirs a significant amount of money and frustration.

I have noticed one major problem with trusts, however: most people don't understand them. When understanding is lacking, trusts may not be handled properly and many of the benefits can be lost. In extreme cases, more problems are created by trusts than are solved by them.

This problem became very apparent to me while assisting several clients with their trust tax returns. During one tax season, fewer than 6% of my clients who were trustees understood their trusts sufficiently to be properly handling them. They had made many mistakes, some of them costly.

When I looked for books to provide guidance to these clients, I made an interesting discovery. There are many books explaining all of the benefits of a trust and how easy it is to set one up. Most of these books were written by attorneys or financial planners who are interested in creating trusts for everyone. Although many of the books covered their material very well, I could *not* find a book written for the average person containing clear, easy-to-understand directions on how to handle a trust once it has been set up. I made it my goal to fill that gap.

I want to make it clear what *The Truth About Trusts* is not. It is not a law book. It does not provide you with legal advice; only your attorney can do that. It does not cover all conceivable situations in which you, as a trustee, may find yourself. (If I tried to do that, you'd never be able to lift this book, and I'd inevitably miss some of the possible scenarios.)

What you *will* find in this book is practical information and procedures which I have developed over the years while assisting my clients in managing their trusts.

The sample letters and checklists are not legal forms; they are guides for you that work. Revise them to meet your particular situation. If your attorney or other advisors recommend that you handle your trust differently, heed their advice.

The purpose of *The Truth About Trusts* is to remove the mystery that surrounds these legal creations. Once you understand trusts, you will see how *easy* and *logical* it is to manage them correctly. It may take a little extra effort, but the results are worth it. You will probably find that understanding and effectively managing a trust requires less effort than you imagined.

One word of caution. Despite the fact that you will learn how relatively simple it is to manage a trust, trust management is not really a "do-it-yourself" project. Make use of your advisors. Your attorney, tax consultant, financial planner, and/or accountant can provide you with valuable insight and direction. Draw on their experience and knowledge to avoid mistakes. The expense of professional advice will generally pay off many times over by resulting in tremendous savings of both taxes and your time.

PART 1

understanding your trust

CHAPTER 1

■ ■ ■ ■ ■ ■ ■ ■

The Creator, the Creation, and the Hired Hand

A Review of Trust Basics

Before getting into the mechanics of operating your trust, it is necessary to review the basic concepts of a trust. This will eliminate misunderstandings when we begin to look at the details. It is important that you understand these basics whether you are thinking about setting up a trust, have already set up your trust, or are now the trustee of someone else's trust. Please remember, this book is not intended to provide you with legal or tax advice. Every trust and every situation is different. Check with your legal, financial, and tax advisors to help determine the best course of action for your needs.

What Is a Trust?

I have found that it is useful to think of a trust in terms of the concept of creation. We, as humans, were given form by our Creator. In turn, we have the capability of creating legal entities called *trusts*.

You can create your trust in almost any form that you desire. Within certain legal boundaries, you can structure your creation to carry out your wishes, even after your death. There is no "standard" trust. Every trust is different. That is why you will see many times throughout this book—READ THE TRUST.

Your trust consists of several characters: the creator, the trustee, and the beneficiary. You will often see these characters called by different titles. Sometimes a role is filled by one individual or organization. Sometimes two or even all three roles are filled by the same individual. That is part of the flexibility you have when you create your trust.

The Creator

Everything begins with the creator of the trust. The creator is called by many different names, all of them valid. Trustor, grantor, trustmaker, and settlor are some of the common names used to distinguish the creator from the rest of the cast of characters. Throughout this book, the descriptive term *trustmaker* is used.

The trustmaker has two basic jobs. The first is to establish the rules that will be followed in operating the trust, including:

1. What assets are to be placed in the trust.
2. How these assets are to be managed.
3. Who will manage the trust.
4. Who will receive income and/or principal from the trust, and under what terms the assets will be distributed.

The second job of the trustmaker is to provide the assets that are to be in the trust. An important part of this job is properly transferring the assets into the trust.

Frank and Ernest

The Hired Hand

You may think of the *trustee* of a trust as a hired hand. This is the individual (or organization, such as a trust department of a bank) responsible for administering the trust in accordance with the rules established by the trustmaker. Throughout this book you will read much more about the duties and responsibilities of this important character in a trust.

During the lifetime of the trustmaker, the trustmaker and the trustee are often the same individual. This allows the trustmaker to retain full control of his or her creation.

The Beneficiary

The assets in the trust are held and administered for the benefit of the *beneficiary*. The beneficiary may receive income and/or principal from the trust, but only under the rules established by the trustmaker. These benefits will be paid out at some time specified by the terms of the trust. The trustmaker has a great deal of control while creating the trust as to when and how these distributions will occur. Often there are several beneficiaries. Sometimes beneficiaries may receive only income, sometimes they may receive only principal, and sometimes they may receive both income and principal. Usually there are restrictions as to when and under what circumstances beneficiaries may receive their benefits.

Revocable vs. Irrevocable Trusts

Often the trustmaker wants to maintain control of the trust assets. In order to allow for changes of circumstances, or even changes of mind, many trusts allow the trustmaker to change the rules after the trust has been created. Assets may be removed or added. The trustee and/or beneficiaries may be changed. Terms of distribution may be modified. The entire trust may be cancelled. If the trustmaker creates a trust that allows these changes, it is called a *revocable trust*.

In general, a trust that does not allow the trustmaker the freedom to make changes is called an *irrevocable trust*. Some irrevocable trusts may allow limited changes under specific terms in the trust.

There are differences in how a trustee must administer the assets, depending on whether the trust is revocable or irrevocable. The IRS, creditors, and Medicaid all treat these two types of trusts differently.

Don't rely upon the name of the trust (for example, "The Smith Revocable Trust") to determine whether the trust is revocable or irrevocable. A trust may start out as revocable, but then become irrevocable due to the death or incapacity of the trustmaker.

Living vs. Testamentary Trusts

The difference between a living trust and a testamentary trust is simple. A *living trust* is one that is set up during the trustmaker's life. A *testamentary trust* becomes operational after the death of the trustmaker, according to the terms of the trustmaker's will or living trust. A living trust may be either revocable or irrevocable. A testamentary trust is irrevocable, since the trustmaker can no longer make changes. A testamentary trust is usually funded as the result of a probate court order.

CHAPTER 2

■ ■ ■ ■ ■ ■ ■ ■

Responsibilities and Perils of Being a Trustee

As the appointed steward of someone's assets, your job is to:

1. Ensure that you are aware of all the assets belonging to the trust.
2. Manage the assets, pay debts, and collect income.
3. File the proper tax returns.
4. Properly account for income and disbursements.
5. Distribute income and principal to the beneficiaries.

Trustees must perform all of these duties in the best interest of the beneficiaries while following the instructions prepared by the trustmaker.

The Trustee as a Fiduciary

The most important thing to remember about your duties as trustee is that you are a *fiduciary*. This means that you have been designated by the trustmaker to act on his or her behalf, solely for the benefit of the beneficiaries. Trustees are held to a higher standard of integrity and responsibility in handling trust assets than in handling their own assets.

Your actions as trustee will be measured by what is known as the "Prudent Investor Rule." This means that you must act in the same manner as a prudent individual would act in managing his or her own assets in similar circumstances. You should avoid unnecessary risks and protect the assets. This does not necessarily mean that you must keep all the money "safely" in the bank. Prudent management may require that you make reasonable investments to protect the purchasing power of the trust.

Trust Assets Do Not Belong to the Trustee

The responsibilities and duties just discussed are all very reasonable and logical. They are things you would want and expect from someone entrusted with your life savings. When you accept the responsibilities of a trustee, you must keep in mind that you are not managing your own funds. These assets belong to someone else (the trust), and are maintained by the trust for benefit of the beneficiaries.

You may or may not keep impeccable records of your own personal finances. A trustee *must* keep current and accurate records of the trust's funds. If a trustee were to die or become disabled, it would be essential that the successor trustee be able to step in and take over without any problems.

You must not commingle trust assets with your own assets, even if you are also the trustmaker and/or the beneficiary. Assets must be kept separate. Do not look upon the trust as a source of short-term (or long-term) loans. Using trust assets for personal benefit would be a violation of fiduciary responsibility. Well-intentioned "paybacks" almost never happen. Even if the money is paid back, a violation of the trustee's fiduciary duty has occurred.

Dangers of Being a Trustee

Many trustees do not realize that when they accept the responsibilities of being a trustee, they may also be accepting a degree of risk related to actions or inactions on their part. If a trustee's imprudent or negligent action results in a loss to a beneficiary, the trustee may have to personally pay back the loss.

The important concept to remember is that the trustee is employed by the trust for the benefit of the beneficiaries. The trustee must not only handle the assets in a prudent manner, he or she must conduct all of the affairs of the trust with a primary objective of being *loyal* to the trust document and its beneficiaries. Confidentiality is of special importance. A trustee must never disclose information about the trust or the beneficiaries to unauthorized persons, nor discuss one beneficiary's affairs with another beneficiary.

Always be watchful for *conflicts of interest.* A typical conflict is any activity that could provide you with a profit to the detriment of the trust. This would include such things as selling an asset to yourself or a friend at a reduced price or for a commission. Conflicts of interest could also occur if you favored one beneficiary over another.

A potential area of personal liability for a trustee is *taxes.* Prudent trustees will file all tax returns and pay all taxes on time. Late filing and payments can create unnecessary expenses (penalties and interest) for the trust. Beneficiaries are entitled to expect reimbursement from a trustee who fails to pay the trust's taxes on time. This includes not only income taxes, but also real estate taxes, personal property taxes, intangible taxes, and motor vehicle fees. If a business is part of the trust, sales and payroll taxes could also be involved.

A trustee may also be *at risk to third parties* due to activities involving the trust. Injuries or other damages caused by trust properties that are not adequately covered by insurance could cause judgments to spill over to the trustee.

Environmental issues can even cause problems for a trustee. The Comprehensive Environmental Response Corporation and Liability Act (CERCLA) of 1980, better known as the Superfund Act, applies not only to major corporations — individuals and trustees can be held liable as well. If you become responsible for real estate — particularly commercial real estate — be sure to promptly check out any potential environmental problems. Leaky gas storage tanks and hazardous waste disposal are two of the more common problem areas.

How to Protect Yourself as a Trustee

With all of these possible pitfalls, you need to be sure you are doing all you can to avoid them. Your best defense is to use common sense. Make sure that your insurance is adequate. Always act prudently. Keep your beneficiaries informed of your actions and results. Avoid potential conflicts of interest. And enlist the assistance of professionals; you are much better off relying on the advice of your attorney, financial advisor, and tax consultant than on your neighbor who was once a trustee.

If possible, become familiar with the terms of the trust before you accept the responsibilities of being trustee. Review all of the assets and liabilities of the trust. Verify that all of the assets are identified and registered in the name of the trust. Investments should be appropriate for the trust in terms of risk and income generation. The needs of the beneficiaries should also be taken into account.

Read the rest of this book carefully. Understand the concepts of a trust. Use the checklists and sample letters. Seek the assistance of professional advisors.

Your duties as a trustee can be successfully completed if you:

1. Understand the terms of the trust.

2. Follow the terms of the trust.

3. *Think through* all decisions.

4. Act prudently.

5. Keep the best interests of the beneficiaries foremost in your mind.

6. Get professional help if you are uncertain about your responsibilities.

CHAPTER 3

■ ■ ■ ■ ■ ■ ■ ■

Choosing Your Hired Hand — How to Select a Trustee

As the trustmaker, you have a significant amount of freedom in creating the terms of the trust. You also have complete freedom in choosing your trustee. Carefully consider this decision. The obvious choice isn't always the best choice.

If you have a revocable living trust, you may not feel that this chapter is important. Since you want to maintain control of your assets, you and/or your spouse will often be the trustee of your trust. That is a shortsighted view. Who will be your successor trustee if you become incapacitated or after you die? Your choice is vital to the proper functioning of your trust after you can no longer control it.

Factors to Consider in Trustee Selection

As has been discussed already, no two trusts are alike. Their purposes may be different, their assets will be different, and the needs of their beneficiaries will be different. In determining who is best suited to manage your trust, consider the following:

1. *Purpose of the trust.* Is your trust designed solely for the purpose of tax reduction, probate avoidance, and easy transfer to your heirs? If so, a friend, relative, or even a beneficiary could serve. On the other hand, if your trust is designed to provide long-term income to one or more beneficiaries, you may want to consider a professional manager or a corporate trustee such as a bank trust department.

2. *Size of the trust.* The larger the trust, the more you should think with your head and not your heart. There is no simple rule of thumb to apply here; just use common sense. Remember, you are entrusting your assets to the trustee for safe and proper management. Larger trusts often require more complex investment strategies.

3. *Duration of the trust.* A short-term trust will very likely be concluded within the lifetime of a named trustee. A longer-term trust may still be in operation after the death or incapacity of your chosen trustee. You must take into consideration the age and health of your trustee.

4. *Assets in the trust.* Make sure that your trustee is capable of managing the assets in your trust. Managing certain kinds of assets requires special skills. For example, if a business is included in the trust, your trustee should have experience with that type of business. Don't assume that your selected trustee knows everything that you know about the trust assets.

5. *Location of the assets.* If your trust consists entirely of bank accounts and investment accounts, the trustee can be located almost anywhere. However, if your trust includes real estate, a business, or any other asset requiring special attention, choosing a trustee who has easy access to the location of the asset may be most prudent.

6. *Identity of the beneficiaries.* In most situations, you would want to choose a trustee who is respected by the beneficiaries, knows the special needs of the beneficiaries, and can work well with them. You don't want a trustee who may be controlled or overpowered by one or more of the beneficiaries, and you don't want a trustee who would be likely to conflict with the beneficiaries. Having the trustee located near the beneficiaries may be a consideration.

7. *Location of advisors.* If you have specified certain advisors to the trust, you may want to choose a trustee who is nearby.

8. *Trustee fees.* Don't name a professional trustee before checking out their fee schedule. You may decide that your trust is too small to warrant their minimum fee. You should also check with any potential non-professional trustee (such as a family member or friend) to determine whether they are willing to serve without receiving a fee or, if not, what fees they would expect. You should reassure any non-professional trustee that they do not have to serve without being paid for their efforts.

9. *Tax considerations.* Check with your attorney and/or tax advisor concerning the tax consequences of your trustee selection. You may lose the tax advantages that you are seeking if you name yourself, your spouse, or a beneficiary as trustee for certain trusts.

What to Look For In a Trustee

As you read the last section on what to consider when choosing a trustee, you may have been thinking about what qualities you want in your trustee. Your choice should be made for practical—not sentimental—reasons.

1. *Trustworthiness.* There are many qualifications needed for a good trustee. The quality of trustworthiness overrides all the others. The very nature of the term "trustee" implies that you are confident that this hired hand will faithfully perform your instructions. If you don't trust your trustee, no matter how competent he or she may be, you have made the wrong choice.

2. *Competence.* This is definitely not a time to let sentimentality rule your decisions. Your favorite child or best friend may be your emotional choice for trustee, but you must make sure that this person is capable of managing the assets. Your trustee must understand both the duties and responsibilities. He or she must be able to make reasonable decisions and be capable of carrying

them out. He or she must be able to recognize situations when professional help is needed, and be willing to seek that help when necessary.

3. *Experience.* You should consider your potential trustee's experience, not only in handling your type of trust assets, but also in managing the complexities of a trust. A well-meaning friend or relative may be trustworthy and competent, but still lack the experience that your trust needs.

4. *Relationship to beneficiaries.* You may desire that your trustee know the beneficiaries and their specific needs. Your trustworthy, competent, and experienced accountant may not have a sufficient relationship with your beneficiaries to make all the best decisions. On the other hand, you may have one or more beneficiaries who will benefit from the distant, impartial control of someone who does not know them personally.

5. *Lack of conflict of interest.* It is often unfair to place the burden of being a trustee on someone who has the opportunity to benefit from their own decisions. Many financial advisors refuse to be trustees in order to avoid any appearance of being self-serving in the way they handle the trust's affairs. Sometimes, if one beneficiary is the trustee, other beneficiaries will make his or her life miserable with accusations that decisions were made to benefit the trustee.

6. *Availability of trustee to serve.* Will the responsibilities be an unbearable burden to the trustee? Your potential trustee could have all the qualities that you desire, but could be already overloaded with work or other responsibilities that would not allow proper attention to the trust activities. Your preferred trustee may have health problems that could make serving difficult, or could be of an age that would make it unlikely that he or she could serve for the full period of the trust. Of course, you may designate one or more successor trustees to alleviate this concern.

Checklist 3-1
SELECTION OF TRUSTEE

Characteristic	Importance	Name of candidate		
Trustworthiness				
Competence				
Experience				
Relationship to beneficiary				
Lack of conflict of interest				
Availability				

Instructions

1. Read the trust.

2. How important to you is each of the listed characteristics? Rate them in the first column as follows:
   a. Extremely important
   b. Important
   c. Neutral
   d. Not important at all

3. Place the name of each potential trustee at the top of a column. Rate each candidate in each of the six characteristics as follows:
   a Excellent
   b. Good
   c. Satisfactory
   d. Unsatisfactory

Review this checklist and determine your best choice.

Making the Decision

In most cases there is probably no *ideal* candidate (other than yourself) for the job of trustee. You will need to weigh the various factors discussed and make your decision based upon what you think will work the best for your trust.

You may find it helpful to use checklist 3-1 to make your decision. This may help you see how your candidates compare with each other. There is no "absolute formula" that will automatically select the best trustee for your trust. Only your good judgment can do this.

One Last Consideration

There is one more very important factor you must consider. Now that you've selected the best trustee, you must make sure that he or she is *willing* to serve. It is foolish to base your plans on a specific trustee, only to find out that this person will not accept the position. This is particularly important if you are choosing a successor trustee to take over upon your death or disability, since you will not have the opportunity to make a different selection.

I am a firm believer that not only should you confirm the willingness of your trustee and/or successor trustee to serve in the designated capacity, but you should also review your trust with them. Make sure they fully understand your desires for the trust, your instructions for the trust, and the various assets in the trust.

Too often, new trustees report that a friend or relative recently died and suddenly they are a trustee—with no idea of what to do or what assets they are expected to manage.

Don't take the chance of your desires being misunderstood by your trustee. This could result in your wishes not being carried out, and possibly higher taxes and fees being paid than necessary.

The best possible scenario is to review your trust with your trustee *and* your financial planner, accountant, and/or attorney present. This can help prevent any misunderstanding of your wishes. As an added benefit, all parties will have the advantage of meeting each other early in the process.

Use of Co-Trustees

Often, trustmakers feel it would be better to have more than one trustee. There are many reasons for this decision:

1. The complexity of the trust and its assets require the talents of more than one trustee to handle the different aspects.

2. The trustmaker may feel that it would be smoother if two or more of the beneficiaries share the duties to prevent conflicts among the beneficiaries. A similar reason is to not show favoritism among the beneficiaries and thus avoid hurt feelings.

3. The trustmaker may want to balance the personal attention of an individual trustee with the judgment, expertise, and impartiality of a professional trustee.

4. One spouse may be better served with the assistance of a third party.

All of these reasons are valid if they fit your situation. Just a word of caution if you are considering more than one trustee or successor trustee. If you choose this option, you have created a committee to manage your trust. This could be cumbersome and cause inefficiencies if the co-trustees disagree on certain courses of action. Each co-trustee shares in the fiduciary responsibilities and has veto power over decisions. Some co-trusteeships work very well, and others have problems.

You know your trust, the trust assets, the beneficiaries, and potential trustees. You must study the situation and make your own decision.

Help! I Just Became a Trustee

You have probably figured out by now that there are three ways you can become the trustee of a trust. You can appoint yourself the trustee of your own trust. You can be appointed the trustee of someone else's trust. Or you can become the successor trustee of a trust due to the death, disability, or resignation of a trustee.

In this chapter, we will concentrate on the second and third scenarios. Handling affairs of your own trust will be covered in detail in Part 3 of this book, which is devoted to the popular revocable living trusts. But don't skip this chapter if you are concerned only with a revocable living trust. Many of the concepts here will also apply to your situation.

Throughout the book, you will find several checklists to help you perform your duties as a trustee. They should be used as a guide in assuming the responsibilities of a trust, operating the trust, and terminating the trust. While I believe the checklists cover most situations, it is still wise to consult with your advisors to make sure you are handling your particular trust correctly.

Some of the action items may not be applicable to your trust. Other items may pertain to your situation, but you may decide not to take action. Consider each item carefully, even if you don't want or need to do anything with it. You may be surprised at some of the things you have forgotten.

You will notice that the first item on every checklist is "Read the trust." Trusts are often very complex documents—written in such detail by lawyers in an effort to cover many details and contingencies—that they can be very difficult to understand. You must take the time to not only read the document, but also to fully understand all of its terms and conditions. Don't ever assume that the trust is simply a "standard" trust. The trustmaker may have been creative with the trust in very subtle ways. You must be sure that you understand the terms of the trust before you can possibly consider following them.

I have often found it useful to diagram the trust in the form of a decision tree flow chart. Figure 4-1 is an example of a basic revocable living trust established by a single individual. This is a very simple example. You will see other examples throughout this book. Most trusts are more complex than this.

Note the basic features identified in each branch of Figure 4-1. The trustee is named. The income and principal beneficiaries are shown. It is clear who is responsible and who receives the benefits.

Figure 4-1
REVOCABLE LIVING TRUST OF JOHN TRUSTMAKER

```
┌─────────────────┐           Yes
│ Is John living? │───────────────────────┐
└─────────────────┘                        │
         │                                  ▼
         │                    ┌──────────────────────────────────────┐
         │                    │ Trust is revocable                   │
         │              No    │ Trustees: John or designated successor│
         │                    │ All income to John                   │
         │                    │ Principal to John                    │
         │                    └──────────────────────────────────────┘
         ▼
┌──────────────────────────────────────┐
│ Trust is now irrevocable             │
│ Trustee: designated successor trustee│
│ Income: per terms of trust           │
│ Principal: per terms of trust        │
└──────────────────────────────────────┘
```

Checklist 4-1
SET UP TRUST — TRUSTMAKER/TRUSTEE DIFFERENT

Action	Trustmaker complete	Trustee complete
1. Read the trust		
2. Notify trustee/trustee acknowledge		
3. Review trust (trustmaker/trustee)		
4. Obtain taxpayer ID number (Form ss-4)		
5. Prepare/acknowledge list of assets in trust		
6. Transfer assets to trust: a. Home		
b. Other real estate		
c. Stocks & bond "house" accounts		
d. Stock certificates		
e. Mutual funds		
f. Limited partnerships		
g. Bank accounts		
h. Loans		
i. Life insurance		
j. Annuities		
k. Other assets		
7. Verify/change beneficiaries: a. Life insurance policies		
b. Annuities		
c. Pensions		
d. Profit-sharing plans		
e. 401(k) plans		
f. Deferred compensation		
g. IRA's		
h. Keogh plans		
8. File Form 56 with IRS		
9. Copy of list/notify of transfer: a. Accountant/tax preparer		
b. Financial advisor		
c. Attorney		

Becoming Trustee of a New Trust

Once you have accepted the responsibilities of being trustee for a newly established trust, you must work with the trustmaker to make sure all necessary forms are filed and all the designated assets are transferred to the trust. Checklist 4-1 will help both the trustee and the trustmaker produce an orderly transition. This checklist is designed as a general guide for you: some items may not be applicable to your trust, and there may be other tasks that will be necessary to fulfill your particular needs.

1. *Read the trust.* Both the trustmaker and trustee must know and understand all of the terms of the trust before attempting to initiate the trust. A flow chart diagram is often very useful in understanding the trust.

2. *Notify the trustee.* The trustmaker needs to notify the trustee and the trustee must acknowledge acceptance of the appointment.

3. *Review the trust.* The trustmaker and trustee should meet to review the trust. Now is the time for the trustee to learn the intent and motivation of the trustmaker. Review the status and location of all assets that will be transferred to the trust. Even though the trustee will be responsible for the management of the assets, a wise trustee will also understand the trustmaker's investment philosophy and goals. Review checklist 4-1 and determine any deletions and additions that are needed. It may be helpful to have your legal, financial, and tax advisor present at this meeting.

4. *Obtain taxpayer ID number.* Since the trust will be a separate taxpaying entity, it must have its own taxpayer ID number. This is easy to obtain by applying to the Internal Revenue Service using Form ss-4. A copy of Form ss-4 is in the appendix (page 236). If your advisors cannot provide you with a copy, you can obtain one by calling the IRS Forms Line toll-free at 1-800-829-3676. You can also download a copy from the IRS Forms website at http://www.irs.gov/forms-pub/forms.html. Don't procrastinate on this. You will need this number for all investments and bank accounts.

You will also need it in order to file tax returns. It normally takes about a week to obtain a taxpayer ID number. During March and April, it will take longer. A separate taxpayer ID is not required for a revocable trust where the trustmaker is also the trustee.

5. *Transfer assets to trust.* You probably won't have all of the different types of assets listed in checklist 4-1, but it is important that you transfer all the necessary assets. Chapter 5 leads you through the transfer procedures for the different type of assets, and includes sample letters to assist you with the transfer process.

6. *Verify/change beneficiaries.* If life insurance policies, annuities, or pension-type assets are involved with the trust, it is important that the correct beneficiaries are named. If changes are needed, you must notify the insurance company or plan custodian. You will find sample letters for this in Chapter 5.

7. *Prepare/acknowledge list of assets in trust.* This is a safety feature for both the trustmaker and the trustee. By having both people check this list, there is a much higher likelihood that all assets have been transferred.

8. *File Form 56 with Internal Revenue Service.* This form notifies the IRS of who has fiduciary responsibility for the trust. You should file it as soon as possible after receiving your taxpayer ID number from the IRS. This form should be filed each time the trustee is changed to keep the information current. A copy of the form is in the appendix (page 237). For revocable trusts that do not require a taxpayer ID number, Form 56 is not necessary.

9. *Provide copies of the asset list.* Even though you have professional advisors involved with the trust, it will save the trust money if you are as organized as possible. If you provide your advisors with a list of the assets, they will have an easier time down the line assisting you in making sure the assets are all accounted for.

PART 2

operating
your trust

CHAPTER 5

■ ■ ■ ■ ■ ■ ■ ■

Transferring Assets
to the Trust

A trust cannot accomplish its intended purpose unless all appropriate assets have been transferred into the trust. In this chapter, you will learn the general transfer concepts and formats. (Transfers to a revocable living trust are covered in Chapter 9.)

A trustee has no authority to administer assets that are not owned in the name of the trust. Assets not titled in the name of a revocable living trust at the time of death must be probated, even if the trustmaker intended to place them in the trust prior to death. Many states do have a provision to allow a small dollar amount of assets not in a trust to escape most of the probate procedures.

Many trustmakers think that they have completed the job when they prepare a list of trust assets and attach it to the trust document. For most assets this isn't the case.

The surest way to transfer real estate to a trust is by recording the proper deed. Without this recorded deed you may have a legally transferred property, but you or your heirs may have to go to court to verify the situation. You have just negated the reason for your trust.

The transfer of securities also requires proper paperwork. There is no legitimate securities transfer agent that will accept a list of transferred assets as proof of transfer. It's much cheaper, faster, and easier to follow the correct transfer procedures than to go to court later to establish trust ownership.

Transfers to a trust are straightforward once you understand the concept. You will discover that the steps you need to take are logical, even if they don't appear that way at first. The transfer process may seem to be time-consuming, but it is much faster and easier than going through probate.

The important thing to remember when doing transfers to a trust is that you are performing an actual transfer of ownership between two different entities. Even when the trustmaker and trustee are the same person, there are two different legal entities. During a transfer, the trustmaker gives or transfers the asset to the trustee, who receives and accepts it on behalf of the trust. (In the case of a testamentary trust, the executor of the estate will usually serve in the role of the trustmaker for making these transfers.)

This chapter contains checklists for the overall transfer as well as transfers of each type of asset. There are also sample letters that you can use to facilitate the transfers.

The sample letters in this and subsequent chapters are not legal forms. The samples have evolved as workable letters as I have helped hundreds of clients complete transfers to trusts. They may

"No, Mrs. Gotrocks, you can't put Mr. Gotrocks in your Living Trust!"

have more attachments or information than is actually needed in a particular case. Since every investment company, transfer agent, and bank has its own procedures, it is common for them to require different documents. I have found that it saves time in the long run to provide "too much" information at the outset than to send incomplete information and have the company write back asking for something else.

The purpose of all of this paperwork is to satisfy all the parties involved that the entity making the transfers is authorized to do so, and that the entity receiving the transfer is the proper entity. The transfer agency also has to comply with various state and federal laws, regulations, and IRS codes when it processes your transfer.

Checklist 5-1 is a general checklist to guide you as you perform your transfers. All actions regarding your trusts require that you read and understand the trust and instructions before proceeding.

Checklist 5-1
TRANSFER ASSETS TO TRUST

Action	Trustmaker complete	Trustee complete
1. Read the trust		
2. Prepare/review list of assets to be transferred		
3. Verify taxpayer ID number		
4. Verify Form 56 filed		
5. Transfer assets per individual checklists		
6. Notify: a. Accountant/tax preparer		
b. Financial advisor		
c. Attorney		

Instructions Before Proceeding

A few other preliminary steps should be taken before actually doing the transfers. First, prepare and review a list of all assets that will be transferred. This way you can make sure that nothing is missed. Checklist 5-2 gives an example of a list of assets.

Having the trustmaker approve each item to be transferred is an added safeguard. The trustmaker has the opportunity to review what is being transferred, and the trustee will have verification that the trustmaker really did want to transfer each asset on the list.

Checklist 5-2
SAMPLE ASSET TRANSFER CHECKLIST

Asset	Trustmaker approval	Paperwork submitted	Transfer completed
Vacant land—Lake Smith			
Home—12234 Main Street			
XYZ mutual fund			
ABC stock			
Stock brokerage account			
CD at local bank			
Gold coins		N/A	
Painting		N/A	

Real Estate

The transfer of real estate normally involves the use of a deed. The current owner or owners sign a deed transferring ownership to the trust. This deed could be a grant deed, warranty deed, or quit claim deed. You should consult your attorney as to the appropriate type of deed for your locality and situation.

You usually can obtain a blank deed from a title company or stationery store. Your local real estate broker may be able to provide you with one. Many attorneys will print out deeds using their word processors.

You will need the current deed as a starting point in this process. The ownership of the real estate will be transferred from the present owner to the new owner (the trust). If all of the owners on the deed are still alive, the transfer will be from all owners, as listed on the current deed. If one or more of the named owners are dead, check with your attorney or title company as to how this should be handled and what additional forms may be required.

The deed should specify that the property is transferred to the trustee of the trust. Name both the trustee and the trust, including the date of the trust. The date is necessary in case you established other trusts with similar names.

An example of a transfer could look like this:

"John Smith and Mary Smith, husband and wife as joint tenants, grant to Harry Smith, trustee of the John and Mary Smith Trust dated July 18, 1999 . . ."

Carefully check the current deed to make sure you are transferring the proper real estate. The current deed contains the legal description of the property. This legal description needs to be on the new deed in exactly the same words. It can be as simple as naming a lot in a recorded subdivision map or as complex as several pages of a surveyor's description.

The signature of the transferor of the real estate should be acknowledged in front of a notary public. Most recording offices require a notary public's signature and stamp before they will record a transfer. Many states require additional forms concerning the status of the transfer. Check with your attorney to verify that you have all of the required paperwork.

Other forms may also be required for recording a valid transfer, depending on the situation. Death certificates, probate orders, and copies of the trust may be required. Your attorney or title company can help you with this.

Before transferring real estate to your trust, you need to check on a few things. How will this affect your mortgage? Will your mortgage holder consider this transfer as a sale to a new owner and call for full payoff of the loan? Will your local government require you to pay a transfer tax? Will your property be reassessed for higher property taxes? When you have a revocable living trust,

Checklist 5-3
TRANSFER REAL ESTATE TO A TRUST

Action	Completed
1. Read the trust	
2. Review current deed	
3. Check with mortgage holder	
4. Check on transfer tax	
5. Check on property tax revaluation	
6. Prepare new deed	
7. Sign/with notary public	
8. Record deed	
9. Notify: Trustee	
Attorney	
Financial advisor	
Accountant/tax preparer	

generally there are no changes to the mortgage or property taxes, but there could be complications when an irrevocable trust is involved. Check with your mortgage company and tax assessor to make sure.

Some trustmakers/trustees prefer to avoid these potential problems by not recording the transfer deed. An unrecorded deed is valid, but since there is no public notice of this transfer, problems could occur later. For example, the property could be mortgaged or sold by the trustmaker without the trustee's knowledge, leading to legal problems.

Due to the complexity of real estate transfer laws and the relatively high value of most real estate, I do not consider the transfer of real estate to a trust a do-it-yourself project. The expense of professional advice in this matter from your attorney or title company is well worth it.

Securities

Along with real estate, securities are the most common type of assets that are transferred to a trust. They include investments such as stocks, bonds, mutual funds, money market funds, brokerage accounts, and limited partnerships.

If you understand the concept of how ownership of these securities is recorded, you will have an easy time in making the transfers. For most of these investments, ownership records are maintained by someone other than you. When you request a transfer to a trust, the organization maintaining the records must make sure that this is a valid transfer. They also need to know how to report income and sales to the Internal Revenue Service.

Sample letter 5-1 is a format I have found effective for transferring *mutual funds, stock brokerage accounts, managed accounts,* and *limited partnerships* to a trust. Your attorney or other advisors may use different letters that are just as effective.

Sample Letter 5-1
TRANSFER MUTUAL FUNDS, MANAGED ACCOUNTS, BROKERAGE
ACCOUNTS, AND LIMITED PARTNERSHIPS TO TRUST

John Smith (as currently registered)
Mary Smith
123 your street
City, state, zip code

Date letter written

(Mutual fund family) (stock brokerage), etc.
Their address
Their city, state, zip code

Ref: (Name of investment), (account number) — (could be more
than one if in same mutual fund/limited partnership family)

Dear Sir/Madam:

I (we) request that the above-referenced account(s) be re-registered
in the name of my (our) trust as follows:

Harry Jones, trustee
Name of trust dated (date you signed trust)
Trustee's address
Trustee's city, state, zip code

The taxpayer identification number for the trust is 12-3456789.

Enclosed are the following:

1. Form W-9 for trust (signed by trustee)
2. (Certified extract of trust) or (appropriate pages from the trust)

Sincerely,   Accepted:

_____   _____
John Smith   Harry Jones, trustee

_____
Mary Smith

* Have signatures Medallion-guaranteed (this is explained on page 35).

The concept is that the current owner is transferring owner-ship to a new owner. The current owner directs the transfer and provides the necessary information to complete the transfer. This information includes:

a. Name of trustee(s)

b. Name and date of trust

c. Address of the trustee

d. Taxpayer identification number of trust

e. Form W-9 verifying taxpayer ID number of the trust (most companies want this for their files). A copy of Form W-9 is included in the appendix (page 238).

f. Verification that this is a valid trust. This could be a two- or three-page condensation of the trust prepared by your attorney and signed by you before a notary public, often called a *certificate of trust* or *certified extract of trust*. If you do not have this, you can usually satisfy the verification requirement by including the title pages of your trust, the page designating the trustee, and the signature page including the notary public's acknowledgment.

Having the trustee accept the transfer by signing the letter next to the trustmaker's signature accomplishes three things. First, there is a record of the requested transfer with the trustee's agreement. Second, the transfer agency is assured that the trustee knows about the transfer. Third, the transfer agency has a record of the trustee's signature.

Most transfers of securities will not be processed without the signatures being "guaranteed." A notary public's acknowledgment will not be accepted. A signature guarantee is a rubber-stamped guarantee with an original signature from a firm participating in the Medallion program. This is usually easy to obtain: most securities broker/dealers, members of stock exchanges, and some banks are members of the Medallion program. A signature guarantee means the guarantor will reimburse the transfer firm for any losses caused by a fraudulent signature. Their guarantee is backed by a bond.

As you look back over the letter and the requirements for transferring securities, you can see the logic in the various steps. Following all of these steps will usually prevent having a letter sent back to you asking for more information and/or additional forms to complete the process. As said earlier, it's more efficient to provide "too much" information up front than to have to follow up later with more.

Limited Partnerships

Sample letter 5-1 will usually accomplish the transfer of mutual funds, stock brokerage accounts, and managed accounts. Limited partnerships often require additional forms and fees. Because of

Checklist 5-4
TRANSFER MUTUAL FUNDS, MANAGED ACCOUNTS, BROKERAGE ACCOUNTS, AND LIMITED PARTNERSHIPS TO TRUST
Name of Asset _____

Action	Completed
1. Read the trust	
2. Write letter (5-1), include attachments	
3. Trustmaker sign (signature guaranteed)	
4. Trustee sign (signature guaranteed)	
5. Mail letter	
6. Complete additional requirements if any	
7. Receive acknowledgment of completed transfer	

various rules restricting the transfer of limited partnership interests and the element of direct ownership of partnership assets, most limited partnerships have their own paperwork requirements for a transfer. Sample letter 5-1 works well as a request for these forms. Most partnerships will use the information that you provide and fill in the forms before sending them to you for signatures, greatly easing the process.

Many partnerships will also require a fee for transfer. The fees are usually in the $25 to $50 range. There is a reasonable basis for charging these fees because of the paperwork involved. Many states require filing or getting permission prior to transfer of limited partnership interests. Some partnerships will waive the fees if the transfer is due to the death of an owner.

Individual Stock/Bond Certificates

There are two methods of maintaining ownership of individual stocks and bonds. Some people prefer to keep the individual certificates in a safe deposit or a file cabinet at home. Others prefer to maintain them in a brokerage account with a securities dealer.

We already learned about the transfer method if you have stocks and bonds in a brokerage account. It is the simple method using sample letter 5-1 with checklist 5-4.

You have more work to do to complete the transfer if you maintain physical possession of your certificates. Most companies do not maintain their own ownership records. With the constant buying and selling of shares it is more cost-efficient to delegate this work to a specialty company, called a *transfer agent,* to perform that function. The transfer agent not only keeps track of who owns how many shares, but is also responsible for mailing dividend checks, proxy ballots, and periodic reports.

In order to transfer your individual stocks and bonds, you must direct the transfer agent for each company to complete the transfer. In addition, you will need to send the stock certificate or bond to the transfer agent so they can cancel the old certificate or bond and issue a new one in the name of the trust.

There are several ways to determine the name and address of each transfer agent. Don't rely on the name of the transfer agent listed on your certificate. Companies often change transfer agents. You can look at the return address on the most recent correspondence (dividend or interest check, proxy, annual report) from the transfer agent. You can contact the company that issued the stock or bond directly and ask for the name and address of the transfer agent from the Investor Relations Department. Or you can have your stockbroker or financial planner look it up for you.

You must enclose the stock certificate or bond with your letter to the transfer agent. Although you have signed the letter of instruction, transfer agents also require that you sign either the back of the certificate/bond or a separate form called a *stock* or *bond power* authorizing the transfer. These signatures must also be Medallion signature-guaranteed.

It is preferable to use the stock power, rather than the back of the certificate. This way you can mail the certificate and the signed power in two separate envelopes, reducing the possibility of loss from theft of the signed certificates. Your broker or financial planner can provide you with a stock power. A sample stock power is in the appendix (page 239).

I recommend that you send these certificates by registered, insured U.S. Mail. As explained shortly, the insurance cost is very small since you only need to insure them for 2% of the value of the stock.

See sample letter 5-2. The CUSIP number is a unique number for each separate class of stock issued by a corporation. It is useful in case you have a certificate from a company which has changed its name, merged with another company, or is no longer in existence. Your broker can use that number to locate the company.

Sample Letter 5-2
TRANSFER STOCK/BOND CERTIFICATE TO TRUST

John Smith (as currently registered)
Mary Smith
123 your street
City, state, zip code

Date letter written

Transfer agent
Their address
Their city, state, zip code

Ref: (Name of corporation), (CUSIP number), (number of shares),
(certificate number(s))

Dear Sir/Madam:

I (we) request that the above-referenced and enclosed certificate(s)
be re-registered in the name of my (our) trust as follows:

Harry Jones, trustee
(Name of your trust) dated (date you signed trust)
Trustee's address
Trustee's city, state, zip code

The taxpayer ID number of the trust is 12-3456789.

In addition to the certificate(s) enclosed are the following:

1. Stock/bond powers (if used)
2. Form W-9 for trust (signed by trustee)
3. (Certified extract of trust) or (appropriate pages from the trust)

Sincerely,   Accepted:

_____   _____
John Smith   Harry Jones, trustee

_____
Mary Smith

* Have signatures Medallion-guaranteed.

39

Checklist 5-5
TRANSFER STOCK/BOND CERTIFICATE TO TRUST
Name of Stock/Bond _____

Action	Completed
1. Read the trust	
2. Locate certificate/bond	
3. Determine transfer agent and address	
4. Write letter (5-2)	
5. Trustmaker sign (signature guaranteed)	
6. Trustee sign (signature guaranteed)	
7. Sign stock certificate/bond/stock power (signature guaranteed)	
8. Mail letter by registered, insured U.S. Mail	
9. Receive new certificate in name of trust	
10. Photocopy certificate	
11. Trustee safely store certificate	

What happens if you have lost your stock certificate or bond? Don't panic—it can be replaced. Your transfer will be delayed. Sample letter 5-3 is an example of how to clear up this matter. Since each transfer agent handles the paperwork differently, you are asking them for their required paperwork.

A transfer agent may require that you post a surety bond to protect them in case your certificate or bond shows up later. The cost of the bond is usually 2% of the value of your lost certificate. This is why I previously recommended that you insure your certificates when mailing them for 2% of the value. The transfer agent will inform you of the exact cost of the bond.

Sample Letter 5-3
TRANSFER LOST STOCK/BOND CERTIFICATE TO TRUST

John Smith (as currently registered)
Mary Smith
123 your street
City, state, zip code

Date letter written

Transfer agent
Their address
Their city, state, zip code

Ref: (Name of corporation), (CUSIP number if known),
(number of shares if known), (certificate number if known)

Dear Sir/Madam:

I (we) are the owners of (number of shares if known) shares in the above-referenced company. I (we) are unable to locate these shares.

I (we) request that these shares be reissued and registered in the name of my (our) trust as follows:

Harry Jones, trustee
Name of trust dated (date you signed trust)
Trustee's address
Trustee's city, state, zip code

The taxpayer identification number of the trust is 12-3456789.

Enclosed are the following:

1. Form w-9 for trust (signed by trustee)
2. (Certified extract of trust) or (appropriate pages from the trust).

I (we) understand that you may require additional forms and a surety bond to complete this transfer. Please forward your requirements to our address above.

Sincerely,   Accepted:

_____   _____
John Smith   Harry Jones, trustee

_____
Mary Smith

* Have signatures Medallion-guaranteed.

Checklist 5-6
TRANSFER LOST STOCK/BOND CERTIFICATE TO TRUST
Name of Stock/Bond _____

Action	Completed
1. Read the trust	
2. Determine number of shares owned	
3. Determine transfer agent and address	
4. Write letter (5-3)	
5. Trustmaker sign (signature guaranteed)	
6. Trustee sign (signature guaranteed)	
7. Mail letter	
8. Receive instructions/forms from transfer agent	
9. Return required letters with check for bond to transfer agent	
10. Receive new certificates in name of trust	
11. Photocopy certificate	
12. Trustee store certificate	

As you write your version of sample letter 5-3 you may not have all the required information. Fill in as much as possible to help the transfer agent identify your account.

I strongly recommend that the trustee photocopy the new certificates before safely storing them (preferably in a safe deposit box). This way the trustee will have a record of the company, number of shares, certificate numbers, and CUSIP number for future reference.

By now, you are probably thinking *there must be an easier way to handle stock/bond certificates!* There is. If you maintain your certificates in a brokerage account, often called holding your shares in *street name,* you can easily transfer the whole account to the trust with one letter (5-1) to the brokerage firm. Using this method there is no danger of certificates being misplaced or lost in the mail, and no effort needed to find the transfer agents to complete your transfer. An additional advantage of maintaining your stocks and bonds in street name is that it simplifies your income tax reporting.

What if you now hold your certificates personally? You can open an account through your stockbroker or financial planner and deposit your certificates with them. Once this is completed, you can follow up by re-registering the account in the name of the trust using letter 5-1.

Checklist 5-7
**ALTERNATE METHOD TO TRANSFER INDIVIDUAL
CERTIFICATES TO TRUST**

Action	Completed
1. Read the trust	
2. Gather certificates	
3. Set up brokerage account	
4. Transfer certificates to brokerage account	
5. Write letter 5-1	
6. Trustmaker sign (signature guaranteed)	
7. Trustee sign (signature guaranteed)	
8. Transfer complete	

IRA's, Pensions, and Other Qualified Tax Deferral Plans

Normally you would not transfer your IRA's, pension/profit-sharing plans, 401(k)'s, 403(b)'s, or other deferred compensation plans to a trust. The major exception to this would be a charitable trust, which we are not discussing in this book. Transfer of one of these tax-deferred plans would normally cause the trust to pay tax on the distribution.

In Chapters 9 and 10 we will discuss these plans within the framework of a revocable living trust. Due to the many different individual situations that may occur, you should consult with your advisors before transferring title of any of these pension-type plans. What you may want to do is change the beneficiary of your plan to the trust. The major difference when compared to transferring an asset is that you do not need the approval of the trustee (new beneficiary). If you name the trust as primary beneficiary, there is generally no need to name a contingent beneficiary. That is because a trust does not die.

Sample letter 5-4 illustrates how to make your trust the primary beneficiary and sample letter 5-5 shows how to make your trust the contingent beneficiary. In the case of letter 5-5, I recommend that you include the full information on your primary beneficiaries even if they are not being changed. This could prevent confusion in the future.

Checklist 5-8
CHANGE BENEFICIARIES OF QUALIFIED PENSION PLAN TO TRUST
Name of Plan _____

Action	Completed
1. Read the trust	
2. Write letter (5-4 or 5-5)	
3. Receive confirmation of change	

Sample Letter 5-4
NAMING TRUST AS PRIMARY BENEFICIARY
OF QUALIFIED PENSION PLAN

John Smith
123 your street
City, state, zip code

Date letter written

Custodian or trustee of your plan
Their address
Their city, state, zip code

Ref: (Type of account), (account number)

Dear Sir/Madam:

I request that the beneficiary designation of the above-referenced account be changed to read as follows:

Primary beneficiary: (Name of trust) dated (date of trust)
Taxpayer identification number of trust: 12-3456789
Contingent beneficiary: None

Sincerely,

*(Have this signature
Medallion-guaranteed.)*

_____
John Smith

(Use the following if the owner of the plan is married).

I am the spouse of John Smith. I approve of this beneficiary designation that does not provide for me as 100% primary beneficiary.

Sincerely,

*(Have this signature acknowledged
before a notary public)*

_____
Mary Smith

If you are married and not making your spouse 100% primary beneficiary, you should have your spouse approve this designation, and have this approval acknowledged before a notary public.

Sample Letter 5-5
NAMING TRUST AS CONTINGENT BENEFICIARY OF QUALIFIED PENSION PLAN

John Smith
123 your street
City, state, zip code

Date letter written

Custodian or trustee of your plan
Their address
Their city, state, zip code

Ref: (Type of account), (account number)

Dear Sir/Madam:

I request that the beneficiary designation of the above-referenced account be changed to read as follows:

Primary beneficiary(s): List all primary beneficiaries — names, addresses, social security numbers, dates of birth, relationship to you, and percentage to each.

Contingent beneficiary: (Name of trust) dated (date of trust)

Taxpayer identification number of trust: 12-3456789

Sincerely,

_____

John Smith

* Have signature Medallion-guaranteed.

Life Insurance Policies

The best way for a trust to take ownership of a life insurance policy is to have the trust purchase the policy. This ensures, if you properly handle your trust, that the death benefit proceeds will not be considered as part of your estate. The ownership of life insurance is not suitable for many trusts and should be carefully considered with the assistance of your advisors.

In this section, we will assume that you have decided to either transfer ownership of an existing policy to your trust, or to name the trust as a beneficiary.

The mechanics of changing the ownership and/or beneficiary of your life insurance policy are similar to the previous ownership/beneficiary changes. The major difference is that most life insurance companies require you to use their forms. You can start the process by either contacting your life insurance agent to request the necessary forms or by writing directly to the insurance company.

Don't request both an ownership change and beneficiary change at the same time, as this will often confuse the insurance company. First change the beneficiary, then change the ownership.

Checklist 5-9
TRANSFER OWNERSHIP/BENEFICIARY OF
LIFE INSURANCE POLICY TO TRUST

Policy #_____ Company _____

Action	Completed
1. Read the trust	
2. Write letter to insurance company (5-6, 5-7, or 5-8)	
3. Complete and return required forms	
4. Receive endorsement of change	

Sample Letter 5-6
TRANSFER OWNERSHIP OF LIFE INSURANCE TO TRUST

John Smith
123 your street
City, state, zip code

Date letter written

ABC Life Insurance Company
Their address
Their city, state, zip code

Ref: Life insurance policy (number) on life of John Smith

Dear Sir/Madam:

I request that the ownership of the above-referenced life insurance policy be transferred to my trust. The owner is:

Harry Jones, trustee
(Name of trust) dated (date of trust)
Trustee's address
Trustee's city, state, zip code

The taxpayer identification number of the trust is 12-3456789.

Enclosed are the following:

1. Form W-9 for trust
2. (Certified extract of trust) or (appropriate pages of trust)

(If premiums are still being paid:)

Please send all future premium notices to the new owner.

Sincerely,   Accepted:

_____   _____

John Smith   Harry Jones, trustee

Sample letters 5-6, 5-7, and 5-8 will help you change owner-ship and the primary or contingent beneficiary of a life insurance policy to the trust. Signature guarantees are not normally required for these changes.

Sample Letter 5-7
CHANGE LIFE INSURANCE PRIMARY BENEFICIARY TO TRUST

John Smith
123 your street
City, state, zip code

Date letter written

ABC Life Insurance Company
Their address
Their city, state, zip code

Ref: Life insurance policy (number) on life of John Smith

Dear Sir/Madam:

I request the beneficiary designation for the above-referenced life insurance policy be changed as follows:

Primary beneficiary: (Name of trust) dated (date of trust)
Taxpayer ID number: 12-3456789
Contingent beneficiary: None

Sincerely,

_____

John Smith

Sample Letter 5-8
CHANGE LIFE INSURANCE CONTINGENT
BENEFICIARY TO TRUST

John Smith
123 your street
City, state, zip code

Date letter written

ABC Life Insurance Company
Their address
Their city, state, zip code

Ref: Life insurance policy (number) on life of John Smith

Dear Sir/Madam:

I request the beneficiary designation for the above-referenced life insurance policy be changed as follows:

Primary beneficiary: List all primary beneficiaries — names, addresses, social security numbers, relationship to you, and percentage to each.

Contingent beneficiary: (Name of trust) dated (date of trust)

Taxpayer ID number: 12-3456789

Sincerely,

_____

John Smith

Annuities

You can use the same letters and checklists for annuities that you use for life insurance policies. You can transfer the ownership to the trust, change the beneficiary to the trust, or do both.

Before making changes or transferring an annuity, review your policy with your financial advisor. Some annuity policies have guaranteed values upon the death of an annuitant and/or owner, as well as the waiver of surrender charges upon the death of an annuitant or owner. Since a trust does not die, your heirs could lose that benefit. Check the wording of your annuity policy and make sure that you understand any benefits that you may be giving up with a transfer of ownership to your trust.

The Internal Revenue Code allows only "natural persons" to accrue earnings in an annuity on a tax-deferred basis. Different annuity companies interpret this in different ways for trusts. Some will report income to the Internal Revenue Service, others will understand that a revocable living trust is owned by a "natural person." Check this out with your tax advisor and the annuity company before transferring an annuity to a trust.

Checklist 5-10
TRANSFER OWNERSHIP/BENEFICIARY
OF ANNUITY TO TRUST
Policy #_____ Company _____

Action	Completed
1. Read the trust	
2. Review policy with advisor	
3. Write letter to insurance company (5-6, 5-7, or 5-8)	
4. Receive endorsement of change	

Bank Accounts

Transferring bank accounts is easy—you are essentially dealing with cash. Since the trust may have a different taxpayer ID number than you do, the bank may require that a new account be established in the name of the trust.

You can take care of this in one of several ways:

1. You can visit your bank with your trustee and have the transfer made directly.

2. You can transfer cash by writing a check to your trust payable to "Harry Jones, trustee, (name of your trust)." Have your trustee open a new account or add to the existing trust account with that check. Your trustee will need a copy of the trust to do this.

3. Have your bank write a cashier's check payable to "Harry Jones, trustee (name of your trust)" and send to your trustee. Have your trustee do the same as in option 2.

Certificates of Deposit

Your bank may not be quite as cooperative with your request to transfer title on a certificate of deposit because there is a little more paperwork for them to do. They probably will go along with you as long as you are not withdrawing your funds. Be sure to verify whether or not the bank will consider this an early withdrawal for the purpose of earning interest and/or charging a penalty.

You can handle this type of transfer using the same concepts as other transfers. I have found that the banks usually have their own forms, particularly signature cards. If your bank is local and easy to get to, make a visit and find out what they require to make a transfer. If not, use sample letter 5-9 to get the ball rolling.

Sample Letter 5-9
TRANSFER CERTIFICATE(S) OF DEPOSIT TO TRUST

John Smith (as currently titled)
Mary Smith
123 your street
City, state, zip code

Date letter written

ABC Bank
Their address
Their city, state, zip code

Ref: Certificate(s) of deposit, (account number) — (list all CD's for this bank on one letter)

Dear Sir/Madam:

I (we) request that you transfer ownership of the above-named certificate(s) of deposit to my (our) trust. Ownership should be listed as:

Harry Jones, trustee
(Name of trust) dated (date of trust)
Trustee's address
Trustee's city, state, zip code

The taxpayer ID number of the trust is 12-3456789. Enclosed are the following:

1. Form W-9 for trust (signed by trustee)
2. (Certified extract of trust) or (appropriate pages of trust)

If any additional forms are required to complete this transfer, please send them to my (our) address above.

If this transfer requires a penalty for early withdrawal or loss of interest, do not complete this transfer. Notify me of any potential penalty.

Sincerely,   Accepted:

_____   _____

John Smith   Harry Jones, trustee

_____

Mary Smith

Checklist 5-11
TRANSFER CERTIFICATE(S) OF DEPOSIT TO TRUST
Bank _____ Account #_____

Action	Completed
1. Read the trust	
2. Visit bank to obtain forms or send letter (5-9)	
3. Complete required bank forms	
4. Receive acknowledgment of transfer	

Untitled Assets

Many of the assets that you desire to transfer to your trust may not have any legal registration of title. This could include such things as gold, stamps, coins, antiques, jewelry, and other personal items. These assets are easy to transfer because no third parties are involved.

If your trust document does not provide for a blanket transfer of these assets, the simplest way is to make a list of the assets you are transferring. State that you are making the transfer to the trust. Have the trustee acknowledge receipt. To ensure that outside agencies (such as the Internal Revenue Service or creditors) respect this transfer, you should have all signatures acknowledged in front of a notary public. Many attorneys include a listing of these assets (often called Schedule A) attached to your trust to accomplish this.

Sample letter 5-10 should guide you through this process if a listing is not attached to your trust.

All of these steps may seem like a lot of work, but they are necessary to properly transfer all the correct assets to your trust. Taken one step at a time, they are logical and relatively easy to complete. After spending hundreds or thousands of dollars preparing your trust documents, don't lose the benefits that you paid for by neglecting this part of the process. The cost is minor, but the benefits are major.

Sample Letter 5-10
TRANSFER UNTITLED ASSETS TO TRUST

John Smith
Mary Smith
Your street address
City, state, zip code

Date letter written

Harry Jones, trustee
(Name of trust) dated (date of trust)
Trustee's address
Trustee's city, state, zip code

Dear Harry:

I (we) transfer to you as trustee of (name of trust) dated (date of trust) for safekeeping and proper management the following assets:

    1. Asset 1
    2. Asset 2
    3. Asset 3 — etc.

Sincerely,

_____   _____
John Smith   Mary Smith

I acknowledge receipt of the above-listed assets and agree to maintain them in accordance with the terms of (name of trust) dated (date of trust).

_____
Harry Jones, trustee

Checklist 5-12
TRANSFER UNTITLED ASSETS TO TRUST

Action	Completed
1. Read the trust	
2. Prepare list of assets	
3. Write letter (5-10)	
4. Transfer custody to trustee	
5. File copy of letter with records	

■ ■ ■ ■ ■ ■ ■ ■ ■

CHAPTER 6

Operating the Trust as Trustee

Up to this point, we have concentrated more on the role of the trustmaker than of the trustee. Once assets have been transferred to the trust, it is time for the trustee to take over and go to work.

The Five Functions of a Trustee

When you break down the various duties of a trustee into the basics, your role as trustee becomes clear. You have only five things to do to fulfill your responsibilities:

1. *Gather the trust assets.* Chapter 5 described the steps for gathering assets from a living trustmaker. In later chapters, you will learn the similar concepts for how to gather assets after the death of the trustmaker.

2. *Manage the assets.* We'll focus on this duty in this chapter.

3. *Prepare reports.* You must keep your employers happy and informed. Reports are required to be given to the beneficiaries and, if appropriate, to the trustmaker. You will learn about these reports in this chapter.

4. *Prepare and file tax returns.* Despite your dislike for this aspect, it is a necessary evil. In Chapter 7, you will learn how to make this thankless task easier.

5. *Make distributions to beneficiaries.* This is often the true purpose of operating a trust. Chapter 12 will guide you through the process.

Trustee as Chief Executive Officer

Earlier, in Chapter 1, the trustee of a trust was described as the "hired hand." That is a valid description, but the job you were hired for is right at the top. If you want to compare the trust structure to that of a corporation, you are the chief executive officer (CEO). You run the show.

Although you are the boss, you do have to answer to the stockholders and board of directors. Depending on the terms of the trust documents, the trustmaker may have the right to replace you. Also, the beneficiaries may have the right, either by terms of the trust or through court action, to replace you.

As trustee it is likely that you are not only the CEO, but you are the *only* employee of the trust. You probably have full responsibility for all aspects of running the trust. Don't be afraid to get assistance from legal, financial, accounting, and tax advisors.

Know the Trust

Your first action as trustee should be to understand the trust. Read it thoroughly. If possible, review it with the trustmaker and answer all of your questions. Consult with your advisors.

Review all the assets that are either (1) in the trust, or (2) coming into the trust. Make sure that you understand the risks, potential rewards, income, liquidity, holding period, withdrawal penalties, tax aspects, and quirks of each asset.

Get to know the beneficiaries. Many trusts leave it up to the discretion of the trustee as to the timing and amounts of distribution from the trust. If this is the case, you must know the special needs, if any, of each beneficiary. You will be required to make fair and impartial judgments that will affect all beneficiaries and the trust assets.

Keeping Records

As the CEO of the trust, you must keep complete records, the same as you would for a business. This applies to the irrevocable portion of a revocable living trust as well as any other trust. You may not keep the best records of your own personal finances. This is your prerogative with respect to your own financial affairs. However, as a trustee, you are responsible for someone else's money and you are *required* to maintain excellent records. This is not a matter of personal choice—it is an absolute requirement.

If the trust includes an operating business, there will probably be extensive financial reports to deal with. Even if the business's bookkeeper or accountant keeps the records and prepares the reports, ultimately you are responsible for their accuracy.

In today's computer age, record-keeping has become greatly simplified and complicated at the same time. Computers can keep track of more data than you may ever find useful. If you are not already familiar with a financial software program such as Quicken, Quickbooks, or Financial Navigator, find somebody who is. Consistent use of one of these programs can be a great help.

Even if you are not computer-literate and have no desire to use computers, record-keeping can be simple and straightforward. There are some basic concepts to follow:

1. You must understand the records.

2. You must be able to explain the records to someone else.

3. The records must be clear enough that someone else could come in, understand them, and take over.

4. The records must be kept up-to-date.

5. The records must be accurate.

6. The records must be complete.

Checking Accounts

One of the assets in just about every trust is a checking account. This account is used to receive income, pay expenses, and make disbursements to beneficiaries.

If this is an active account with lots of transactions, you may want to consider using a software program like Quicken to keep track of your activity. If you will be writing checks only occasionally, the "old-fashioned" system of a manual checkbook ledger will be sufficient.

Always keep the trust's checking account separate from your personal account. Do not try to keep a separate subaccount record within your own checking account. This is not your money. Some trustees prefer to keep the trust's money in a different bank than their own personal funds to avoid any chance of commingling. Be sure to print the trust's name on the checks and deposit slips for identification purposes. It is helpful to use a unique check design or color to distinguish the trust account from other accounts.

Remember to keep checking account fees as low as possible. Part of your fiduciary responsibility is to keep costs down. The trust is responsible for normal fees and check printing costs. You could be held personally responsible for unnecessary fees such as overdrafts.

If you are not going to be writing a lot of small checks for the trust, you may want to consider establishing a money market mutual fund as your checking account and/or reserve account. This way you can earn a reasonable amount of interest and have no fees. The major disadvantage of a money market fund is that it is not FDIC-insured. However, I know of no losses historically in this type of fund. Be sure to find out if there is a minimum dollar amount allowed for checks: some have a minimum of $100, others have minimums of $250 to $1,000. Make sure that your needs fit their requirements.

Investments

The approach to handling investments in the trust will depend upon the purpose of the trust. If the primary purpose is to transfer the assets of the trust to the beneficiaries as soon as possible, you will probably not need to be concerned with many investment decisions. On the other hand, if the purpose of the trust is to provide long-term growth in value and/or ongoing income to the beneficiaries, the investments will require active management.

Trust assets are managed using the principles of the Prudent Investor Rule, which means that investment decisions follow what a prudent investor would do in similar circumstances. This does not mean a trustee must produce the highest possible return, as that would often require too much risk. At the same time, it may be imprudent to invest solely in insured certificates of deposit (CD's) that restrict the return that you can make. Depending on your trust's objectives, you must balance risk and reward.

You should develop a plan that meets the specific needs of your trust. An investment advisor can be an important ally in this effort. Many trust documents authorize, encourage, or require professional assistance in this area.

Investment record-keeping is normally very simple. Many software packages have modules that do it for you almost automatically. In general, I recommend that you maintain the following records:

a. *A folder for each investment.* You can keep reports received about each investment in a separate folder. Statements reporting values, dividends, interest, purchases, and shares should be kept in chronological order for easy reference. All correspondence (to you and from you) related to this asset belongs in this folder.

b. *Asset listing.* Keep a list of all the assets. Periodically calculate the value of each asset and post it to this list. This way you can tell at a glance the value of the trust. If you don't use a software package, just use paper with several columns so you can spot trends. Figure 6-1 is a simple example.

c. *Income statement.* Each year it will be necessary to calculate the income earned by the trust and report it to the Internal Revenue Service on the tax return. We will discuss taxes in the next chapter. It is helpful to be able to see the trust's income during the year to plan any distributions to beneficiaries and to plan for taxes. If you have maintained a separate file on each investment, it is easy to periodically list the income from each investment. Figure 6-2 gives an example.

d. *Expense Statement.* If you don't use a computer, your checkbook record will normally give you an easily accessible record of the expenses, but you will need to categorize the expenses for your reports. Choose the categories of expenses that make sense for your trust. Figure 6-3 is an example of an expense statement developed using the expenses listed on the Form 1041 fiduciary tax return.

e. *Receipts.* You should maintain a file folder of receipts for each year as proof of your expenses. For ease in reporting and review for any audits, keep these receipts categorized by the type of expense shown on your reports, not by date.

Special Record-Keeping Hints

If your trust includes a business or real estate rental, maintain a separate checking account for each business and possibly each rental. This will simplify your record-keeping and tax reporting.

Most mutual fund statements show all activities that have occurred to date for that year. If that is the case, you need to retain only the last statement you receive for the year. This will greatly reduce the volume of your files.

It is always better to have an excess of records than not have something you need. When in doubt, keep the paper!

Figure 6-1

ASSET LISTING

Investment	1/1/98	7/1/98	1/1/99	7/1/99	1/1/00
Cash					
Checking account	$1,050.75	$975.15	$1,125.30	$1,200.80	$605.14
CD (First Natl. Bank)	5,000.00	5,100.00	5,202.00	5,306.04	5,412.16
Mutual Funds					
ABC Stock	21,107.60	22,162.98	21,719.72	24,326.08	23,109.78
JKL Intl.	15,401.54	16,633.66	16,966.34	19,171.96	19,229.48
XYZ Bond	8,419.49	8,675.59	8,846.04	8,757.58	9,020.37
Stocks					
BCD Mfg.	1,400.00	1,330.00	1,356.60	1,359.31	1,466.76
Total Assets	$52,379.38	$54,877.38	$55,216.00	$60,121.77	$58,843.69

Figure 6-2

INCOME STATEMENT
Year-to-Date as of June 30, xxxx

Investment	Income
CD – First National Bank	$100.00
ABC Stock Fund	210.08
JKL International	0.00
XYZ Bond	410.14
BCD Manufacturing	70.00
Total Income	$790.22

Figure 6-3

EXPENSE STATEMENT
Year-to-Date as of June 30, xxxx

Interest:		
Bank of Washington	$ 25.00	
Total Interest		$ 25.00
Taxes:		
Property taxes	2,000.00	
Income taxes:		
IRS	1,000.00	
State of California	250.00	
Total Taxes		3,250.00
Fiduciary fees:		
Harry Jones, trustee	1,000.00	
Total Fiduciary Fees		1,000.00
Charitable contributions		0.00
Attorney, accountant & tax return preparer fees:		
Thomas Jefferson, Attorney	250.00	
George Harris, Tax Preparer	250.00	
Total Attorney, Accountant & *Tax Return Preparer Fees*		500.00
Other expenses:		
Postage	22.50	
Office supplies	35.05	
Investment advisory	1,410.10	
Total Other Expenses		1,467.65
Total Expenses		$6,242.65

64

Making Reports

Review your trust document to determine how often and to whom you need to make reports. Informed trustmakers and beneficiaries are usually much happier than uninformed ones. If annual reports are required, the best time to do this is when you prepare the income tax return. You already have the information readily available.

As a minimum, these reports should include the current asset listing, income statement, expense statement, and detailed listing of all cash receipts and disbursements. You, your advisors, and/or the beneficiaries may desire additional reports.

CHAPTER 7

■ ■ ■ ■ ■ ■ ■ ■

Income Taxation
of Your Trust

Income tax law has a major effect on how trusts are written and how they are operated. Taxes can be owed or not depending on how you handle your trust. This chapter will deal with the concepts of taxation of trusts and will provide you with guidelines to reduce the tax burden and keep you out of trouble. It is not intended to provide you with comprehensive tax advice, nor is it a line-by-line guide for filling out the tax forms—that is beyond the scope of this book. The *basic* Internal Revenue Service instructions for filing Form 1041 contain 27 pages of small print. To make sure that you are filing a correct return, you need an experienced tax advisor. However, if you understand the concepts of taxation, you will be able to make the proper decisions throughout the year.

Which Trusts Are Required to File a Tax Return?

Not all trusts have to file a tax return. Most revocable living trusts are set up in a manner where the trustmaker, trustee, and beneficiary are all the same people. The trustmaker still has full control of the assets. All investments and bank accounts still use the trustmaker's social security number for reporting purposes. Since all income is reported on the trustmaker's personal tax returns, a separate tax return is not required. We will discuss the revocable living trust fully in Part 3 (Chapters 8–11) of this book.

A trust tax return is required whenever a fiduciary relationship has been established. All irrevocable trusts will have to file a trust tax return. A trust tax return is required for the irrevocable portion of a revocable living trust after the death of the first spouse. A revocable living trust where the trustee is a different individual than the trustmaker should file a trust tax return since there is now a fiduciary relationship.

Preliminary Steps

In Chapter 4, you learned about the need for and how to obtain a taxpayer ID number for your trust. This number is needed not only to properly transfer assets to the trust, but also to file the trust's tax return. To receive a taxpayer ID number you need to file Form SS-4 with the Internal Revenue Service. A copy of Form SS-4 is included in the appendix (page 236). Do this well in advance of the deadline for filing your tax return. The Internal Revenue Service tends to slow down as April 15 approaches.

As trustee, you also should file Form 56 with the Internal Revenue Service informing them of your fiduciary status. This was also discussed in Chapter 4. A copy of Form 56 is included in the appendix (page 237).

The Concept of Trust Taxation

The taxation of trust income is based on the same basic structure as your individual income tax. The trust reports its income and subtracts its deductions to determine taxable income. It uses tax tables with rates currently ranging from 15% to 39.6% to determine its federal income tax.

Tax Rates

Congress has always been concerned that trusts might be used to reduce the total income taxes that we pay. If someone in a high income tax bracket shifts income to a trust that is in a lower bracket, there could be a tax savings. Congress doesn't like that, especially if this is the sole or primary reason for establishing the trust.

Congress solved this by adjusting the tax brackets so that a relatively low level of trust income is taxed at a relatively high rate. As you can see in Table 7-1, tax rates are much more favorable for individuals than trusts. This schedule is for 1999 only; the tax rates are adjusted annually for inflation.

States that tax personal income also tax trust income.

Table 7-1
FEDERAL INCOME TAX RATES (1999)

Tax Rate	Taxable Income		
	Trust	Single	Married Joint
15.0%	$ 0 – 1,750	$ 0 – 25,750	$ 0 – 43,050
28.0%	$1,750 – 4,050	$25,750 – 62,450	$43,050 – 104,050
31.0%	$4,050 – 6,200	$62,450 – 130,250	$104,050 – 158,550
36.0%	$6,200 – 8,450	$130,250 – 283,150	$158,550 – 283,150
39.6%	$8,450 –	$283,150 –	$283,150 –

Taxation of Trust Distributions

There is a way around these high trust rates. In general, tax law allows a trust to deduct all income that is distributed to beneficiaries from its taxable income. By making distributions you can greatly reduce or even eliminate taxes paid by the trust.

As you are doing your planning in this area, it is important that you understand the rules. They are not always straightforward and could trap you into paying unnecessary taxes if you are not aware of them. Even though they are not straightforward, there is logic behind them.

The amount that you distribute to beneficiaries is not necessarily deductible as distributed income. The tax codes have coined a phrase, *distributable net income* (DNI). This is the amount of distributions made that can be considered distributions of *current* income. Distributions in excess of DNI are considered to be distributions of principal or previously taxed trust income. The basic calculation of DNI is:

Total taxable earnings
- Deductions
- Capital gains
+ Tax-free interest
= Distributable net income

The first two items in the calculation are familiar concepts. The trust is like a business. It has income that is subject to tax. It is allowed to deduct expenses from this income. This is straight-forward logic.

For distribution purposes, capital gains usually are considered as principal, not income. At first this may not seem logical, but it is. Here is an example. Assume that your trust owned a piece of real estate that cost $100,000. You sell the real estate for $150,000, a $50,000 capital gain. If you distribute that capital gain to the beneficiaries, you have reduced the principal of the trust by $50,000. The $50,000 capital gain was not "earned." It was an increase in value.

A few trusts contain instructions to distribute capital gains as income. Most trusts either direct that capital gains be retained by the trust or are silent in this matter. This is another good reason to READ THE TRUST.

Tax-free interest, such as municipal bond or tax-free bond fund interest, has to be added into the determination of the total DNI. This income is not included in total taxable earnings because it is not taxable.

There is a significant reason for including tax-free interest in the calculation of DNI. Your trust receives a deduction for all income distributed to beneficiaries. However, there is no deduction for tax-free interest that is distributed. When calculating the income distribution deduction, you have to prorate the deduction for the portion that comes from tax-free interest. For example, if total income for the trust was $7,500 taxable income and $2,500 tax-free interest, the DNI would be $10,000. If $8,000 were distributed to beneficiaries, the income distribution deduction would be:

$$\$8,000 \times \frac{\$7,500 \text{ taxable income}}{\$10,000 \text{ DNI}} = \$6,000$$

Look back at Table 7-1. When you compare the trust tax rates with the individual tax rates, you will understand why it is important to distribute as much trust income to the beneficiaries as possible if your goal is to reduce taxes. Be sure to read the trust to determine if you are allowed to distribute income, required to distribute income, or required to retain income in the trust. You must follow those instructions.

One problem often occurs with making the proper DNI distribution. You will usually not know the exact amount of income earned by the trust before the end of the year. Reports from investments may not be received until sometime after December 31. You may not have completed your accounting of all expenses.

You have some leeway to take care of this problem. Section 663(b) of the Internal Revenue Code allows you to make deductible distributions up to 65 days after the end of the year. This allows time to determine the year-end results and make distributions in an orderly manner. If you use this 65-day grace period, you have to check a box on page 2 of your Form 1041 tax return that says "If this is a complex trust making the Section 663(b) deduction, check here." This keeps the records clear in case of a future audit.

Other Tax Deductions

Just like your personal tax return, you are able to deduct many of the trust's expenses. Unlike your return, there is *no standard deduction.* You must itemize the deductions. The rules regarding trust deductions are similar to your personal deductions.

Any expenses involving business, farm, or rental income are reported on separate schedules for those activities. The deductions reported in the deduction section are those involved with the operation of the trust itself.

Interest Deductions

For most cases, interest that would have been deductible on your personal return is deductible on a trust return. Interest you normally could not deduct on your own Schedule A is not deductible on the trust return.

Non-deductible interest includes revolving charge accounts, personal notes, installment loans on personal use property, and underpayment of taxes.

Interest on investment purchases, as well as interest on loans needed to operate the trust and its property, is deductible. Interest on a home is deductible if it is the primary residence of a beneficiary. As a practical matter, a residence inherited by a trust that is now vacant is considered an investment of the trust. Interest on this inherited residence would be deductible as investment interest.

Taxes

You can deduct the same taxes as you would on your personal return. These include state and local income taxes and property taxes (both real and personal). You can also deduct any generation-skipping transfer tax that has been imposed on income distributions.

Taxes that are non-deductible include federal income tax; estate, inheritance, legacy, succession, and gift tax; federal duties and excise tax; and sales tax.

Fiduciary Fees

Most trusts allow the trustee to be paid a "reasonable compensation" for administering the trust. These fees are deductible as an expense of operating the trust.

The lure of being compensated for your efforts is both strong and logical. As trustee, you need to consider all factors before paying yourself a fee. You may or may not want to do this.

Any trustee fees paid to you are taxable to you as ordinary earned income. If your trustee duties involve active participation in the operation of a business or extensive management activities over a long period of time, the Internal Revenue Service could consider your trustee activities as self-employment. This would require you to pay self-employment tax, in addition to income tax on your fees. Self-employment tax pays your social security and Medicare taxes, at twice the rate normally paid by employees. (Since there is no employer to pay the other half, you pay both halves.)

If you are the sole income beneficiary, you may want to consider foregoing any fiduciary fees and increasing the trust distribution of income instead. You will receive the same income, but not be subject to self-employment tax. You may also be taxed on less income. As you will learn later in this chapter when Schedule K-1 is discussed, only net taxable income that is distributed to beneficiaries is taxable. Any principal or tax-free income is not taxed. You could find decreasing your compensation and increasing your distribution to be very advantageous tax-wise.

On the other hand, if you are not a beneficiary or if there is more than one beneficiary, it is probably both smart and appropriate to pay yourself trustee fees. You deserve to be compensated for the effort you make and the responsibilities you bear as trustee.

Reimbursement for expenses that you incur as trustee is a different story. You should always keep records of these expenses and have the trust reimburse you. You will not have to pay taxes on these documented expense reimbursements. The trust will still be able to deduct these expenses. Included in these expenses would be mileage at the Internal Revenue Service allowable rate, other travel expenses, as well as out-of-pocket expenses.

Attorney, Accountant, and Tax Preparer Fees

Again, read the trust. Most trust documents authorize and often encourage the trustee to seek professional advice. Do it. This investment will pay dividends. It will probably save you time, money, and headaches.

As you have learned from this book, the concepts of trusts are simple. Thanks to Congress and the laws they pass, the implementation of your trust may not be so simple. Unless you have had the experience of administering several trusts, you will probably make errors. Errors can cost the trust, and you, unnecessary taxes. Poor investments can cost the trust income and growth. Improper administration may cause upset beneficiaries, lawsuits, and personal liability to you as trustee.

Spend the money for professional assistance. You get it at a discount because it is deductible. It is very possible that this assistance will save you more than it costs. It certainly will make your life easier.

Charitable Contribution Deductions

On your own personal return, you can deduct contributions to charity and governmental organizations. You can do the same with trust contributions if they are permitted by the trust.

Be careful. Most trusts cannot make charitable contributions. Remember, you are following the orders of the trustmaker. Your desires, and the desires of the beneficiaries, do not matter. The trust can only make contributions if the terms of the trust authorize or require them. Read the trust.

Proration of Deductions—Taxable/Non-Taxable Income

You may find that you cannot deduct all of the expenses of the trust. You are required to prorate all expenses that are involved with the production of both taxable and non-taxable income according to the proportion of taxable income to the total income.

Examples of the types of deductions that would be prorated are investment management fees, fiduciary fees, and miscellaneous deductions. The percentage would be calculated using the following formula:

$$\text{Allowable deduction} = \frac{\text{Taxable income}}{\text{Taxable income} + \text{tax-exempt interest}} \times \text{Total deduction}$$

What Is Tax-Free Income?

Not all income that avoids tax is considered tax-free income in calculating your income distribution deduction and prorating your other deductions. In this context, tax-free means interest from municipal bonds and municipal bond funds.

Earnings within deferred annuities are not tax-free earnings. Normally, we think of annuities as producing tax-deferred income that will be eventually taxed whenever it is withdrawn. Annuities owned by a trust may be treated differently. Tax deferral of annuity earnings is only allowed for "natural persons." Trusts may or may not be considered natural persons. Different life insurance companies have given me different interpretations as to whether or not they would report current earnings to the Internal Revenue Service for annuities owned by a trust. In general, annuities owned by a revocable trust for the benefit of the trustmaker are considered to be owned by a natural person. Annuities owned by an irrevocable trust may or may not be considered to be owned by a natural person. Check with your tax advisor and the life insurance company's legal department before placing an annuity within a trust.

The trust may also receive other cash flow that is not fully counted as income. A portion of cash from real estate is sheltered by depreciation deductions. The same is true for equipment leasing investments. In reality, depreciation is a deferral of income as it is "recaptured" when the property or equipment is sold.

Some of the cash from oil and gas investments is also free of taxes. This is because as you remove oil and gas from a well you are actually depleting your asset. That is why a depletion allowance is given to allow you to recover your initial investment.

Gifts to a trust or contributions of additional property by a trustmaker are not considered income.

Schedule K-1, Tax Reporting to Beneficiaries

Earlier you learned that the trust did not have to pay income tax on income that was distributed to beneficiaries. That is because the beneficiaries are required to pay tax on their share of the income that they receive. As you saw in Table 7-1, the tax rate schedule is usually higher for trusts than for individuals, making it worthwhile to transfer the tax consequences from the trust to the beneficiaries, if possible.

Schedule K-1 is used to report this transfer of tax liability, both to the beneficiary and the Internal Revenue Service. The income is reported based upon the type of income within the trust. Interest is reported as interest, dividends as dividends, rental income as rental income. In this manner, each beneficiary reports the appropriate amount of each type of income earned by the trust.

Remember, not all distributions to beneficiaries are taxable. Some will be tax-free as discussed earlier. Some may be distributions of the principal of the trust and not taxable. No more than the net taxable income of the trust has to be reported to the beneficiaries.

Look at the following example. Assume that the only income of the trust was $1,000 in interest. The trustee determines that $900 will be distributed to the beneficiaries. The trust had deductible expenses of $300 for the year. The net distributable income for the trust is $700 ($1,000 interest less $300 expenses). Even though the beneficiaries received $900, only $700 is reported as interest income on their Schedule K-1.

Exemption

On your individual return, you are allowed a deduction for each exemption that you claim. In 1998, that exemption was $2,700 for each dependent. Your trust also receives an exemption. For simple trusts, where all the income is required to be distributed to the beneficiaries, that exemption is $300. All other trusts have a $100 exemption.

When to File Your Trust Tax Return

All trusts are required to report their taxes based on a calendar year ending December 31. Trust tax returns are due to be filed by April 15 unless you request an extension.

Don't wait until April to start preparing your return. That is too late. If your trust distributes its income each year to reduce the taxes owed by the trust, that distribution must be made within 65 days of the year-end. You cannot make the proper distribution without knowing the trust's net income. In order to do this, you need all of the information necessary to prepare and file your return. You might as well complete the job early and get it over with.

There is another good reason for preparing the return as soon as possible. If you have made distributions to beneficiaries, they need their Schedule K-1's in order to file their own returns. You will have unhappy beneficiaries if you make them wait until the last minute to file their returns because they have not received their K-1 from you.

State Tax Filings

So far, we have considered just the federal tax implications of trusts. Each state also has rules regarding taxation of trust income. Each trust will be governed by the tax rules of the state in which the trust is administered. This means that the location of the trustee determines the state tax filing requirements for the trust.

In addition, each beneficiary is responsible for reporting his or her share of the income (as reported on Schedule K-1) on their state income tax return. They may also have to report their share of business or real estate income to the state where that income was generated.

Estimated Tax Filings

Trusts are required to pay their taxes in a "timely" manner, the same as individuals. This may cause you to make estimated tax payments using Form 1041-ES, similar to estimated tax payments required by individuals.

In order to avoid a penalty for underpayment of estimated taxes, you generally need to pay in, on a quarterly basis, one of the following:

a. All but $1,000 of the current year's tax liability.
b. 90% of the current year's tax liability.
c. 100% of the previous year's tax liability.

Failure to do this can result in a penalty and potential breach of your fiduciary responsibilities.

Each state has its own estimated tax requirements.

Some trustees prefer—and some trusts may require the trustee —to make estimated tax payments on behalf of beneficiaries for the tax liabilities resulting from trust distributions. These payments are reported on Schedule K-1.

My experience has been that estimated payments made by the

trustee on behalf of beneficiaries tend to confuse the Internal Revenue Service. Even though they are reported on Schedule k-1 and Schedule k-1 is attached to the individual beneficiary's tax return, the Internal Revenue Service often will not recognize these payments as having been made. It sometimes requires many letters to the Internal Revenue Service and much frustration to straighten things out.

It is better to coordinate with your beneficiaries and work with them on filing their own estimated tax payments to remove this potential confusion. The trust can provide additional distributions to cover these tax payments, if necessary. I've found this method to work much better with less confusion, than having the trust make estimated payments on behalf of the beneficiaries.

Checklist 7-1
TAX PREPARATION CHECKLIST

Action	Completed
1. Read the trust.	
2. Review list of all assets.	
3. Ensure all 1099's/k-1's received from each appropriate asset.	
4. Make final income distributions prior to 65 days from year-end.	
5. Prepare tax return.	
6. Deliver k-1 statements to each beneficiary as soon as possible.	
7. File tax return prior to April 15 unless you have requested an extension.	
8. Place tickler on your calendar to pay any required estimated tax payments throughout the coming year.	

Checklist 7-1 will help guide you each year as you prepare the trust's tax returns.

Tax Summary

Each trust is its own individual tax reporting entity. The tax laws have been written to discourage build-up of assets within a trust. (The relatively high tax rates at low income levels encourage distribution of income to beneficiaries).

Trust tax laws, although fundamentally logical, are more complex than individual tax laws. The trustee should consult with a competent tax professional who is experienced with trust returns. Many years ago I thought that trust tax returns were not very difficult to prepare. Then I took several courses on trust taxes and realized their true complexity.

the revocable
living trust

CHAPTER 8

■ ■ ■ ■ ■ ■ ■ ■

What Is a Revocable Living Trust?

The revocable living trust is one of the most common, least understood, and therefore most often misused estate planning tools available. It is an extremely useful and efficient mechanism for transferring assets to your heirs and potentially reducing estate taxes upon your death.

Unfortunately, most people who set up a revocable living trust do not understand what they have created. They often feel that once they have established a trust, everything is taken care of. This is not the case. In reality, after you sign the trust documents, pay your attorney fees, and bring the massive volume of paperwork home, you have a worthless pile of papers. It is only after properly implementing your trust that it becomes valuable to you.

In this chapter we will review what a revocable living trust is and what it can do for you. Chapters 9 through 13 will guide you and your successor trustees through the steps required to put your trust to work for you.

Once you understand the basics of your trust and what must be done to manage it, you will find that your task is both logical and relatively easy to perform.

A revocable living trust is just like the other trusts you have read about in the first two sections of the book. It is the creation of a legal entity used to hold title to assets. There are the same

three characters: trustmaker, trustee, and beneficiary. These characters are often the same individual or individuals.

As its name implies, it is *revocable*. As long as the trustmaker is alive and competent, he or she can make changes to the trust. The trustee and the beneficiaries can be changed. The terms of the trust can be changed. Assets can be added or removed from the trust. The trustmaker can completely dissolve the trust. All of the property truly belongs to the trustmaker.

It is a *living* trust because it was created during the lifetime of the trustmaker.

Avoiding Probate With a Revocable Living Trust

When someone dies, all of their assets will be transferred either to their heirs, to a charity, or to the government in the form of taxes. Some of the assets may be automatically transferred to another person who already owned part of the asset as a joint tenant. Other assets will easily transfer due to a contract that had been set up. An example of this is life insurance benefits passing to a named beneficiary.

Most of the other assets will often be more difficult to transfer. The title to real estate is normally recorded at the County Recorder's Office so that a buyer can verify that he is purchasing from the true legal owner. Stocks, bonds, and other securities are usually registered with a transfer agent to ensure good title. The legal procedure to transfer most of these assets after a death is called *probate*. A judge will review the assets, make sure all debts and taxes are paid, allow time for disputes to be settled, and then declare the new ownership according to the terms of the will if there was one, or according to state laws if the person died without a will. Then the assets can be transferred.

It is advantageous to avoid probate due to the time, cost, and hassles involved. Assets that are owned by a revocable living trust do not have to go through probate. Since the trust is an entity separate from the trustmaker, it doesn't die. When the trustmaker dies, the trust still owns the assets.

One of the trust provisions should name a successor trustee to assume the duties and responsibilities of the trustee upon the death (or incapacity) of the original trustee. The successor trustee can then take control of the assets of the trust, manage these assets according to the terms of the trust, and disburse them to the ultimate beneficiaries as dictated by the trustmaker in the trust document. No courts, attorneys, or judges are needed for this.

A simple revocable living trust might be diagrammed like the example in Figure 8-1.

Figure 8-1
SIMPLE REVOCABLE LIVING TRUST

Is trustmaker alive?

Yes

All income to trustmaker.
Trustee is trustmaker.
Trust is fully revocable by trustmaker.

No

Trustee is the named successor trustee.
All income and principal goes to named beneficiaries according to terms of trust.
Trust is irrevocable.

Reducing Estate Taxes With a Revocable Living Trust

The second benefit of a revocable living trust is its potential to reduce and often eliminate estate taxes for a married couple's heirs. If the trust is properly written and properly handled, your heirs may be able to receive hundreds of thousands of dollars after your death that may otherwise have taken a one-way trip to Washington, D.C.

Current tax law allows each of us to transfer to anyone we choose a certain amount of our assets without paying any type of transfer tax. These transfers can occur either before death as gifts, after death as inheritances, or as a combination of those two ways. The tax-free transfer amount, called the *unified credit amount,* was increased by the Taxpayers' Relief Act of 1997 from $600,000 to $1,000,000 in several steps as follows:

Year of Transfer	Tax-Free Transfer Amount
1997	$ 600,000
1998	625,000
1999	650,000
2000–2001	675,000
2002–2003	700,000
2004	850,000
2005	950,000
2006 & later	1,000,000

In addition to these limits, you can transfer an unlimited amount to your spouse without any transfer tax.

The only problem with transferring all of your assets to your spouse upon death is that when he or she dies later on, only one estate tax exclusion amount is available to your heirs. The exclusion amount of the first spouse to die has been lost.

Most revocable living trusts for married couples are designed so that the exclusion for the first spouse to die is not lost. This is accomplished by splitting the estate into two or more trusts. One trust is the surviving spouse's trust and is still revocable. The assets in the second and subsequent trust(s) are removed from the surviving spouse's estate by making those trusts irrevocable for the benefit of the ultimate heirs.

The effect of this splitting of the assets is to allow a portion of the estate to be "taxed" upon the first death because it is not being transferred tax-free to the surviving spouse. As long as the value on the date of death does not exceed the exclusion amount, there is no tax on the assets in this trust. This irrevocable trust is a separate legal entity from the surviving spouse. It is not a part of the surviving spouse's estate, and does not die when the surviving spouse dies. Upon the death of the surviving spouse, there is no estate tax upon any of the assets in this trust, no matter how large the value of the assets may be at that time.

This may not seem to be a good idea for the surviving spouse to lose a portion of his or her assets just to save estate taxes for the heirs. The assets in the irrevocable trust(s) may be needed for adequate support or even for the enjoyment of the surviving spouse. This is often provided for by allowing the surviving spouse to be the trustee of this trust as well as the income beneficiary and limited principal beneficiary of this trust. The result is that the surviving spouse has given up neither the control nor the benefit of these assets. What the surviving spouse normally cannot do is change the ultimate beneficiaries of the trust.

Figure 8-2 is a diagram of a typical revocable living trust that is designed to reduce estate taxes. While this example is typical of many revocable living trusts, it does not represent *all* revocable living trusts. Trustmakers have the right to create their trust to best suit their own needs and desires. Do not fall into the trap of believing you are working with a "standard" trust. **READ THE TRUST.**

Figure 8-2
THE JOHN & MARY SMITH FAMILY TRUST
Typical Revocable Living Trust Designed to Reduce Estate Taxes

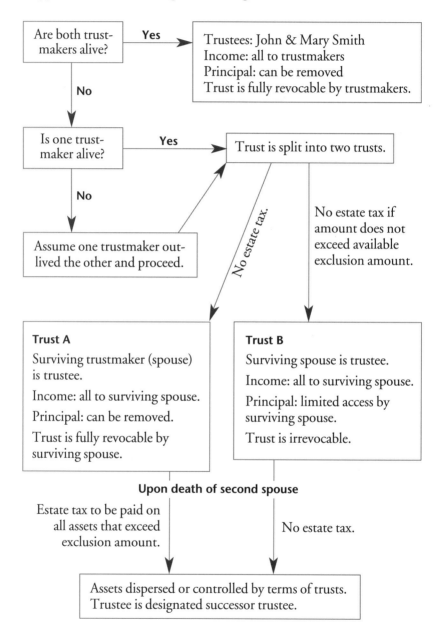

Taxation of Revocable Living Trusts

In Chapter 7, we discussed the concept of taxation of trusts. Most revocable trusts are taxed directly on the tax return of the trustmaker. Since the assets in the trust can be removed at any time by the trustmaker, they truly belong to the trustmaker. There has been no fiduciary relationship established. All income is reported in the social security number of the trustmaker(s).

Once all or a portion of the revocable trust becomes irrevocable the situation changes. The irrevocable trust must now file a tax return. Chapters 7 and 11 give you the details.

Common Mistakes With a Revocable Living Trust

Revocable living trusts are truly strange creatures. They are very easy to handle correctly if you understand them and take appropriate action. You can also very easily lose the benefits and advantages of a trust you created by making one of the errors below. The list that follows describes common and easily avoidable mistakes. Avoid them!

1. *Not transferring all assets into the trust.* After reading Chapters 5 and 9 you know how relatively easy this task can be. Yet many people will invest in the creation of their trust and never actually transfer some or all of their assets into it. They should have saved their money.

2. *Buying new assets without registering them in the name of the trust.* There is no easier time to place an asset in your trust than at the time you buy it. When you buy real estate or any other investment, you have to fill in your name on a form. It is just as easy to fill in your name as the trustee of your trust at that time. This seems simple and logical. However, I have had clients who, having set up a trust, made subsequent investments in their own name instead of registering them in the name of their trust. Following the person's death, transferring the assets that had been properly placed in the trust was easily accomplished without

89

probate. However, transferring those assets that had not been placed in the trust required the involvement of a lawyer and additional paperwork. Be sure that you title all new assets in the name of the trust. Minor mistake, costly correction.

3. **Transferring real estate out of trust for refinancing purposes and not transferring it back.** Most lenders do not understand trusts and refuse to lend on properties owned by a revocable living trust. As a result, most trustmakers are forced to transfer real estate back to themselves, personally, in order to complete the refinance. At that point, many people forget to transfer the property back to the trust.

4. **Not understanding the terms of the trust.** It is always amazing when a client comes to me and says, "I have a living trust, but I don't know what it means." Trusts are often written in complex legal terms supposedly designed to prevent confusion. They often cause confusion. Make sure you understand the terms of the trust before you sign it. Read it periodically so you continue to understand it. If questions come up, ask your attorney, financial planner, or tax consultant to make sure you understand. You won't be able to follow the terms of the trust, and reap its benefits, if you don't understand your trust.

5. **Not educating your spouse and successor trustees.** This problem is similar to the previous one. Both spouses need to understand the features of the trust. Nobody knows who will be the surviving spouse and have the administrative responsibilities after the first death. Don't add this extra burden to a surviving spouse. It is also unfair to place this burden on the shoulders of a successor trustee without preparing them beforehand.

6. **Not following up on the split of assets after the first death.** The estate tax savings aspect of your trust will be lost if your estate is not properly split after the first death. This seems very logical, but many surviving spouses "don't want to bother" with the details. We will discuss this fully in Chapter 10.

7. *After a split of assets upon the first death, not taking the income from the irrevocable trust portion.* As discussed in Chapter 7, the tax rates for trusts are much higher than for individuals. You should make sure that, as a surviving spouse, you take income from the irrevocable trust to reduce the overall tax burden. This will be discussed in greater detail in Chapter 10.

8. *Not filing tax returns for the irrevocable trust after a split.* This usually results from not understanding the workings of a trust. If no tax returns are filed, the Internal Revenue Service could contend that no trust split occurred and that all assets stayed in the estate of the surviving spouse. This could greatly increase the estate tax that would have to be paid when the surviving spouse dies later on.

CHAPTER 9

■ ■ ■ ■ ■ ■ ■ ■ ■

Transferring Assets to a Revocable Living Trust

When you leave your attorney's office after signing the paperwork that establishes your revocable living trust you will probably feel very good about completing an important step in your estate planning. However, you shouldn't feel too smug. You really haven't *completed* anything—you have simply taken a very significant step forward.

To complete the creation of your trust, you must transfer all the necessary assets to the trust. I emphasized the importance of this step in both Chapters 5 and 8. Your trust does not do one bit of good for you, your spouse, or your heirs until the transfers are complete. A trust without assets is as worthless as an automobile without gasoline. It looks good but gets you nowhere.

The transfer procedures for a revocable living trust are similar to those in Chapter 5. There are some subtle but significant differences. Rather than constantly refer you back to Chapter 5, all the necessary checklists and sample letters for transferring your assets to your revocable living trust are included again in this chapter.

Some attorneys will include a blanket transfer of assets with your trust documents. This may be a valid backup in case some items do not get officially transferred. However, do not rely on this document to satisfy all transfer agencies after your death. Follow through and complete the actual transfer paperwork.

Transfer Concepts

The transfer of an asset to a revocable living trust is somewhat strange. Even though the ownership name is different, in many ways there is no transfer of ownership. You still have full control of the asset. The income is reported to the Internal Revenue Service using your social security number. You pay the income tax on the earnings. Usually, you don't even have to file a trust tax return. You can take back the asset from the trust at any time you desire.

Even though it may not be a true, full transfer of ownership, it is very important that all intended assets are transferred properly to your trust. Otherwise, you have wasted your money. Assets not properly titled in the trust's name will probably have to be probated after your death.

The transfer process is the same as the transfer to an irrevocable trust. You, as the trustmaker (and owner of the property) transfer all required assets to the trust. The trustee (usually you) accepts the assets into the trust.

Many assets, such as real estate, securities, and bank accounts have their titles recorded with third parties. This way a record is kept to prove ownership. For real estate, it is important that the public recording agency is notified of your changes in ownership. For securities (stocks, bonds, and mutual funds) the transfer agency must acknowledge and accept the transfer. Life insurance companies and banks usually handle their own re-registration of ownership.

There is paperwork involved. It is *simple*, but it must be done correctly. If you use the checklists that follow and adapt the sample letters to your needs, you will find that your job is straightforward. It may be tedious, but it is logical.

As mentioned earlier, the checklists and letters are not legal documents. Over the years, I have found that they will do the job. Your advisors may have others that will work just as well.

Coordination With Your Successor Trustee

It is not required that you notify the individual(s) or organizations designated as your successor trustee of any transfers that you are making. You don't even have to notify them that you have a trust or that you have named them successor trustee after you become incapacitated or die. Many trustmakers do not feel comfortable letting others know what they are doing. This is often the case when the successor trustee is one of the ultimate beneficiaries of the trust.

While there may be good reasons for not letting your successor trustee know what is happening, it is preferable to keep them informed. This way your successor will know your desires and be familiar with the assets in the trust. It is strongly recommend that you keep your successor informed to the fullest extent that you feel comfortable.

Starting the Process

Checklist 9-1 is a general guide to assist you with the transfers. This checklist is a little different from checklist 5-1. There is no need to verify the trust's taxpayer ID number or file Form 56, since you are using your own social security number. There is no fiduciary relationship established if you are the trustee for your own assets. You don't have to notify your accountant or tax preparer because you are not affecting your tax return. And there is only one column to check for completion of each item since you are both the trustmaker and the trustee.

After reading your trust, the next step is to prepare a list of assets that you want to transfer. Checklist 9-2 is a sample asset transfer checklist. There are no untitled assets in the checklist. Most revocable living trusts include a clause that makes a blanket transfer of these items as well as a schedule for listing these assets. For practical purposes, it would usually be too difficult to maintain an up-to-date list of every single asset that you own.

Checklist 9-1
TRANSFER ASSETS TO REVOCABLE LIVING TRUST

Action	Completed
1. Read the trust	
2. Prepare list of assets to be transferred	
3. Transfer assets per individual checklists	
4. Notify: a. Financial advisor	
b. Attorney	
c. Successor trustee	

Checklist 9-2
SAMPLE ASSET TRANSFER CHECKLIST

Asset	Paperwork submitted	Transfer complete
Vacant land—Smith Lake		
Home—1234 Main Street		
XYZ Mutual Fund		
ABC Stock		
Stock brokerage account		
CD at local bank		

When you initially prepare checklist 9-2 be sure to leave room for additional items. It is very likely that you may miss something the first time through. You may also find that this checklist is handy for adding new items whenever you invest in new assets that are titled in the name of the trust. You can also cross out assets that you have sold or no longer own.

Real Estate

When you transfer your home or other real estate to your living trust, you follow the same procedures that you would to transfer real estate to a completely separate entity. You, as the current owner, sign a deed transferring the real estate to you, as the trustee of your trust. This could be a grant deed, warranty deed, or quit claim deed. You should consult your attorney to determine the appropriate type of deed to use for your situation and locality.

You can obtain a blank deed from a title company or a stationery store. Check with your local real estate broker for help with this. Many attorneys will handle this transfer as part of preparing your trust. They usually can print out deeds directly from their word processors.

Use your current deed as the starting point for this transfer. You need to know how the title is held, since the transfer must be written describing the current owner in exactly the same way you are holding title. The second reason for starting with your current deed is that you want to describe the property being transferred using exactly the same legal description that appears on your deed. This way there is no question about your property being in your trust.

The deed for the transfer must indicate that you, the current owner, are transferring the property to you, the trustee of your trust. The date of the trust must be included in case you previously established other trusts or in case you create additional trusts in the future.

An example of the wording of a transfer on the deed could look like this:

"John Smith and Mary Smith, as joint tenants, grant to John Smith and Mary Smith, trustees of the John and Mary Smith Family Trust dated July 19, 2000, . . ."

Many attorneys in community property states prefer to transfer a joint tenancy asset into community property before transferring it into the trust. This way it is clearly held as a community property asset in the trust, allowing for a full step-up in basis upon the first death.

You should sign this deed in front of a notary public and have your notary acknowledge your signature. Most recording offices require a notary's signature and seal before they will record your transfer.

Your transfer will be valid even if you do not record it. Some trustmakers may prefer not to record the transfer to the trust, as they do not want to make public record of their trust. They may also want to avoid notifying the local assessor of a "change in ownership," opening the door for an attempt to revalue their property for property tax purposes or even a transfer tax. Most localities recognize the reality that a transfer to a revocable living trust is not a change in the true ownership and will not increase your assessment. Just in case, it is best to check this possibility before recording.

I recommend that you do record this transfer. It will make it much easier for your successor trustees. An unrecorded deed may be valid, but a misplaced unrecorded deed, or an unrecorded deed that nobody knows about, is worthless.

You may run into one problem after you have transferred your property to your revocable trust. If you refinance, your new lender may require you to take the property out of the trust. Many banks and other lenders want to make their loans only to "real people" and not to trusts. This is really no big deal. The escrow company handling the refinance can prepare a deed transferring the property back from the trust to you. After your new loan is funded, all you have to do is prepare another deed transferring the property back to your trust.

Checklist 9-3
TRANSFER REAL ESTATE TO REVOCABLE LIVING TRUST

Action	Completed
1. Read the trust	
2. Review current deed	
3. Check on transfer tax	
4. Check on property tax revaluation	
5. Prepare new deed	
6. Sign (with notary public)	
7. Record deed	
8. Notify: a. Attorney	
b. Financial advisor	

Securities

The transfer of securities such as stocks, bonds, mutual funds, money market funds, brokerage accounts, and limited partnerships is usually easier than transferring real estate. It is often taken care of with a simple letter and sometimes a follow-up form.

As long as you keep straight the various participants involved with the transfer, you'll understand what needs to be done and why, the procedures will make sense, and you will have an easy time completing your transfers.

The first participant in this transaction is you, the trustmaker. As the current owner of the asset, you must be the one who requests the transfer. The transfer letter must come from you and be signed by you.

The second participant is the trustee. Your security is being transferred to the trust in care of the trustee. Usually you are both the trustmaker and the trustee. This may seem to be wasted effort, if you are both the trustmaker and the trustee, but I like to have the trustee also sign the letter accepting the asset into his or her (in reality, your own) care in the trust. This verifies to anyone reviewing the transaction that you understand that the trust is a separate entity. It also avoids having the letter returned with a request for the trustee's signature if a legal department feels it is necessary.

Let's call the third participant the transfer agent. This is the organization responsible for keeping track of ownership of the shares of stock, mutual fund, or whatever type of security is involved. It could be the issuing company or governmental agency. Or it could be an independent third party who has been hired to keep track of the ownership of shares. You address your letter to this transfer agent requesting the transfer. The agent will verify that it has received all the necessary information for the proper recording of ownership—such as name, address, and taxpayer ID number—as well as verify that your trust is a valid legal entity. They will also need assurance that it really is the trustmaker who is requesting the transfer.

The last member of this cast is the Internal Revenue Service. The IRS must be informed whenever a security provides you with taxable income and whenever you sell the security. This is why you must provide the transfer agent with the taxpayer ID number that will be used by the trust.

Sample letter 9-1 is a format I have found to be effective for transferring mutual funds, stocks, brokerage accounts, managed accounts, and limited partnerships to a revocable living trust. As you review this letter, notice that the current owner has requested a change in ownership of the asset and has provided all of the necessary information and documentation to establish the new

Sample Letter 9-1
TRANSFER MUTUAL FUNDS, BROKERAGE ACCOUNTS, MANAGED ACCOUNTS, AND LIMITED PARTNERSHIPS TO REVOCABLE LIVING TRUST

John Smith (as currently registered)
Mary Smith
Your street address
City, state, zip code

Date letter written

(Mutual fund family, stock brokerage, etc.)
Their address
Their city, state, zip code

Ref: (Name of investment) (account number) — (could be more than one if in same mutual fund/limited partnership family)

Dear Sir/Madam:

I (we) request that the above-referenced account(s) be re-registered in the name of my (our) revocable living trust as follows:

John Smith and Mary Smith, trustees
(Name of your trust) dated (date you signed trust)
Trustee's address
Trustee's city, state, zip code

The taxpayer identification number will remain my social security number: 123-45-6789.

Enclosed are the following:

1. Form W-9 (signed by you, but listing the owner's name as the trust).

2. (Certified extract of trust) or (appropriate pages from the trust).

Sincerely,   Accepted:

_____   _____

John Smith   John Smith, trustee

_____   _____

Mary Smith   Mary Smith, trustee

* Have signatures Medallion-guaranteed.

ownership. The new owner, the trustee, has accepted the ownership responsibilities. Your intentions are clearly spelled out. Even the Internal Revenue Service would have to acknowledge the validity of the transfer.

The Medallion signature guarantee for these securities transfers serves a similar function as a notary acknowledgment serves for a real estate transfer. A disinterested third party witnesses your signature and certifies that you really did sign the letter of instructions. Securities transfer agents will require this signature guarantee and will not accept a notary acknowledgment. The guarantee protects the transfer agent from liability in case of fraudulent transfer. There is a bond backing the guarantee to reimburse the transfer agent for any costs involved to correct a transfer that used an improper signature. This signature guarantee is easy to obtain from most securities dealers and members of stock exchanges, and some banks.

Checklist 9-4
TRANSFER MUTUAL FUNDS, BROKERAGE ACCOUNTS, MANAGED ACCOUNTS, AND LIMITED PARTNERSHIPS TO REVOCABLE LIVING TRUST

Name of Asset _____

Action	Completed
1. Read the trust	
2. Write letter (9-1)	
3. Trustmaker sign (signature guaranteed)	
4. Trustee sign (signature guaranteed)	
5. Mail letter	
6. Complete additional requirements if any	
7. Receive acknowledgment of completed transfer	

Occasionally, there may be additional requirements to complete a transfer to your trust. A few companies require their own paperwork. Once in a while, they may request that the pages of your trust be certified as current, correct, and in full force. This certification must be made within 60 days of the company's receipt of your letter. This can usually be completed for you by your attorney.

Checklist 9-4 is useful to keep track of the transfers you have in process.

Limited Partnerships

Limited partnerships are transferred in the same manner as stock accounts, mutual funds, and other securities accounts. Sample letter 9-1 is the way to start the process. Because of various rules governing the transfer of limited partnerships and the element of direct ownership of partnership assets, most limited partnerships have their own set of forms that they will require you to sign. My experience has been that the majority of limited partnerships will fill in these forms from the information you provide in letter 9-1 and send them back for you to sign, often requiring another signature guarantee.

Expect to pay a fee for this transfer. Because of the necessary paperwork and filing requirements in some states, the limited partnership transfer fee is warranted. The fee is normally between $25 and $50 to reimburse the partnership for their transfer costs.

Individual Stock/Bond Certificates

If you keep your stock and bond investments in a brokerage account with your stockbroker or financial planner, the transfer to your revocable trust is accomplished simply by using sample letter 9-1 and checklist 9-4. If you keep your stock certificates in a safe deposit box or a file cabinet at home, you have a little more work to do to complete your transfer. Instead of transferring ownership of all your stocks or bonds with one letter, you must transfer ownership in each company separately.

Most companies do not maintain their own records of who owns shares in their company. With the constant buying and selling of shares, it is more cost-efficient to farm out this work to a specialty company, called a *transfer agent,* to perform that function for them. This transfer agent not only keeps track of who owns how many shares, but is also responsible for mailing dividend checks, proxy ballots, and periodic reports.

In order to transfer your individual stocks and bonds you must direct the transfer agent for each company to complete the transfer. In addition, you will send the stock certificate or bond to the transfer agent so they can cancel the old certificate or bond and issue a new one in the name of the trust.

There are several ways to determine the name and address of each transfer agent. Do not rely on the name of the transfer agent listed on your certificate. Companies often change agents. You can look at the return address on the most recent correspondence (dividend or interest check, proxy, or annual report) from the transfer agent. You can contact the company directly and ask for the information from the Investor Relations Department. Or you can have your stockbroker or financial planner look it up for you.

You must enclose the stock certificate or bond with your letter to the transfer agent. Even though you have signed the letter of instruction, transfer agents also require that you sign either the back of the certificate/bond or a separate form called a *stock* or *bond power* authorizing the transfer. These signatures should also be Medallion signature-guaranteed.

It is usually preferable to sign the stock power rather than the back of the certificate. This way you can mail the certificate and the signed powers in two separate envelopes, and reduce the possibility of loss from theft of a signed certificate. Your broker or

Sample Letter 9-2
TRANSFER STOCK/BOND CERTIFICATE
TO REVOCABLE LIVING TRUST

John Smith (as currently registered)
Mary Smith
Your street address
City, state, zip code

Date letter written

Transfer agent
Their address
Their city, state, zip code

Ref: (Name of corporation), (CUSIP number), (number of shares), (certificate number(s))

Dear Sir/Madam:

I (we) request that the above-referenced and enclosed certificate(s) be re-registered in the name of my (our) revocable living trust as follows:

John Smith and Mary Smith, trustees
(Name of your trust) dated (date you signed trust)
Trustee's address
Trustee's city, state, zip code

The taxpayer identification number will remain my social security number: 123-45-6789.

In addition to the certificate(s), enclosed are the following:

1. Stock/bond powers (if used)
2. Form W-9 for trust (signed by trustee)
3. (Certified extract of trust) or (appropriate pages from the trust)

Sincerely,   Accepted:

_____   _____

John Smith   John Smith, trustee

_____   _____

Mary Smith   Mary Smith, trustee

* Have signatures Medallion-guaranteed.

financial planner can provide you with a stock power. A sample stock power is located in the appendix (page 239).

Send these certificates by registered, insured U.S. Mail. The insurance cost is very small, since you only need to insure them for 2% of the value of the stock.

Sample letter 9-2 can be used to transfer your stock and bond certificates to your revocable trust. The CUSIP number is found on your certificate; it is used to identify stocks and bonds issued by a corporation. You can use this number to track down the

Checklist 9-5
TRANSFER STOCK/BOND CERTIFICATE
TO REVOCABLE LIVING TRUST

Name of Stock/Bond _____

Action	Completed
1. Read the trust	
2. Locate certificate/bond	
3. Determine transfer agent and address	
4. Write letter (9-2)	
5. Trustmaker sign (signature guaranteed)	
6. Trustee sign (signature guaranteed)	
7. Sign stock certificate/bond/stock power (signature guaranteed)	
8. Mail letter by registered, insured U.S. Mail	
9. Receive new certificate in name of trust	
10. Photocopy certificate	
11. Safely store certificate	

company that issued a certificate if it has changed its name or merged with another corporation. Your broker can help you use the CUSIP number to find your company if you haven't heard from them in a while.

Use checklist 9-5 to guide you in transferring each certificate to the trust.

Lost Stock Certificates or Bonds

What happens if you have lost your stock certificate or bond? Don't panic—it can be replaced. Your transfer will be delayed. Sample letter 9-3 is an example of how to clear up this matter. Since each transfer agent handles the paperwork differently, this letter asks them for their requirements.

They will require that you post a surety bond to protect them in case your certificate or bond shows up later. The cost of the bond is usually 2% of the value of your lost certificate. This is why I previously recommended that you insure your certificates when mailing them for 2% of the value. The transfer agent will inform you of the exact cost.

As you write your version of letter 9-3, you may not have all the required information. Fill in as much as possible to help the transfer agent identify your account.

Now that you have gone through all of this work to obtain your newly re-registered stock certificates, there is one more step you should take before storing them securely in your safe deposit box. Take a few minutes and photocopy your new certificates. This way you will have an accurate backup record of the company, number of shares, certificate numbers, and CUSIP numbers for future reference. Here's another hint to make it easier for future trustees of your trust: store your certificates in the envelope in which you received them, so your successor trustee will have information on who issued the certificate (and when).

Sample Letter 9-3
TRANSFER LOST STOCK/BOND CERTIFICATE
TO REVOCABLE TRUST

John Smith (as currently registered)
Mary Smith
Your street address
City, state, zip code

Date letter written

Transfer agent
Their address
Their city, state, zip code

Ref: (Name of corporation), (CUSIP number if known), (number of shares if known), (certificate number if known)

Dear Sir/Madam:

I (we) are the owners of (number of shares if known) shares in the above-referenced company. I (we) are unable to locate these shares.

I (we) request that these shares be reissued and registered in the name of my (our) revocable living trust as follows:

John Smith and Mary Smith, trustees
(Name of your trust) dated (date you signed your trust)
Trustee's address
Trustee's city, state, zip code

The taxpayer identification number will remain my social security number: 123-45-6789.

Enclosed are the following:

1. Form W-9 for trust (signed by trustee)
2   (Certified extract of trust) or (appropriate pages from the trust).

I (we) understand that you may require additional forms and a surety bond to complete this transfer. Please forward your requirements to our address above.

Sincerely,   Accepted:

_____   _____
John Smith   John Smith, trustee

_____   _____
Mary Smith   Mary Smith, trustee

* Have signatures Medallion-guaranteed.

Checklist 9-6
TRANSFER LOST STOCK/BOND CERTIFICATE TO TRUST
Name of Stock/Bond _____

Action	Completed
1. Read the trust	
2. Determine number of shares owned	
3. Determine transfer agent and address	
4. Write letter (9-3)	
5. Trustmaker sign (signature guaranteed)	
6. Trustee sign (signature guaranteed)	
7. Mail letter	
8. Receive instructions/forms from transfer agent	
9. Return required letters/forms with check for bond to transfer agent	
10. Receive new certificate in name of trust	
11. Photocopy certificate	
12. Store certificate	

There Must Be An Easier Way!

There is an easier way to handle the re-registration of bonds and stock certificates into the name of your trust. You already learned how, if you keep your securities in a brokerage account, you can transfer ownership using sample letter 9-1.

If you personally hold your certificates, consider opening a brokerage account with your financial planner or stockbroker. Turn your certificates over to this account. Now you don't need to worry about your certificates being lost in the mail or in your filing system. You don't need to know who the transfer agent is for each stock. Once your stocks are in your account, you can use one letter (9-1) to transfer the entire account into your trust's name. Once this transfer has been completed, you have the option of requesting that certificates be issued to you in the name of the trust. However, by now you probably have learned the benefits of leaving the certificates in the brokerage account.

Checklist 9-7 will guide you through this alternative process.

Checklist 9-7
ALTERNATE METHOD OF TRANSFERRING INDIVIDUAL CERTIFICATES TO REVOCABLE LIVING TRUST

Action	Completed
1. Read the trust	
2. Gather certificates	
3. Set up brokerage account	
4. Transfer certificates to brokerage account	
5. Write letter (9-1)	
6. Trustmaker sign (signature guaranteed)	
7. Trustee sign (signature guaranteed)	
8. Transfer complete	

IRA's, Pensions, and Other Qualified Tax Deferral Plans

You will not transfer your IRA's, pension/profit-sharing plans, 401(k)'s, 403(b)'s, or other deferred compensation plans to your revocable living trust. Transfer of one of these tax-deferred plans would be considered a distribution, eliminating its tax-sheltered status and causing you to pay tax on the distribution.

This doesn't mean that you should completely ignore these plans as you establish your revocable living trust. You may want to name your trust as a beneficiary for ease in the final distribution of your assets. This is not an automatic decision, however; there are many reasons not to name your trust as a beneficiary.

If you are married, there is a major benefit to naming your spouse as primary beneficiary. Current tax law allows a spouse to maintain the tax-deferred status of these pension-type accounts until he or she actually receives the benefits. Often this is accomplished by rolling over the account into an IRA in the name of the spouse. The full value remains as an asset of your spouse without a reduction for income tax. Since the beneficiary distribution of these benefits is done by a contract, no probate is necessary. All estate distributions to a spouse are free of estate tax.

Unless there is a specific personal reason for not naming your spouse as the primary beneficiary, such as a commitment to children of a previous marriage, most married couples find that naming their spouse is the best choice for primary beneficiary.

It might make the most sense to name your revocable living trust the contingent beneficiary if you are married, or possibly the primary or contingent beneficiary if you are single. But, as just discussed, the choice is not automatic. Review your options with your financial advisor before making this decision.

Distributions of pension-type plans to a trust are subject to income tax for the year of distribution. This tax will be paid by the trust, or by the beneficiaries if there has been a timely distribution to them. Review Chapter 7 for the tax consequences of a trust. Unlike a transfer to a spouse, the income taxes can no longer be deferred.

A named beneficiary, other than your spouse, does have limited tax deferral options. They can defer receipt of the distribution for up to five years. They can also choose to receive the benefits as a monthly or annual income based upon life expectancy rather than receiving the distribution and paying income taxes all at once. Very few beneficiaries choose these options, but they may have no choice if the plan pays directly to your trust.

It is up to you how you want your pension, IRA, or other pension-type account distributed. Evaluate your options before deciding whether to name your trust as the beneficiary.

Sample letter 9-4 illustrates how to make your revocable living trust the primary beneficiary, and sample letter 9-5 shows how to make your trust the contingent beneficiary. In the case of letter 9-5, I recommend that you include the full information on your primary beneficiaries even if they are not being changed. This could prevent future confusion.

If you are married and not making your spouse 100% primary beneficiary, you should have your spouse approve this designation. (This approval should be acknowledged before a notary public.) Many plans and several states require this spousal approval.

Sample Letter 9-4
NAMING REVOCABLE LIVING TRUST AS PRIMARY
BENEFICIARY OF QUALIFIED PENSION PLAN

John Smith
Your street address
City, state, zip code

Date letter written

Custodian or trustee of your plan
Their address
Their city, state, zip code

Ref: (Type of account), (account number)

Dear Sir/Madam:

I request that the beneficiary designation of the above-referenced account be changed to read as follows:

Primary beneficiary: (Name of trust) dated (date of trust)

Taxpayer ID number of trust: Remains as my social security number: 123-45-6789

Contingent beneficiary: None

Sincerely,

_____   *(Have this signature*
John Smith   *Medallion-guaranteed.)*

(If appropriate:)

I am the spouse of John Smith. I approve of this beneficiary designation that does not provide for me as 100% primary beneficiary.

_____   *(Have this signature acknowledged*
Mary Smith   *before a notary public)*

Sample Letter 9-5
NAMING REVOCABLE LIVING TRUST AS CONTINGENT
BENEFICIARY OF QUALIFIED PENSION PLAN

John Smith
Your street address
City, state, zip code

Date letter written

Custodian or trustee of your plan
Their address
Their city, state, zip code

Ref: (Type of account), (account number)

Dear Sir/Madam:

I request that the beneficiary designation of the above-referenced account be changed to read as follows:

Primary beneficiary(s): List all primary beneficiaries — names, addresses, social security numbers, relationship to you, and percentage to each.

Continent beneficiary: (Name of trust) dated (date of trust)

Taxpayer ID number of trust: 123-45-6789

Sincerely,

_____   *(Have this signature*
John Smith   *Medallion-guaranteed.)*

(If appropriate:)

I am the spouse of John Smith. I approve of this beneficiary designation that does not provide for me as 100% primary beneficiary.

_____   *(Have this signature acknowledged*
Mary Smith   *before a notary public)*

Checklist 9-8
CHANGE BENEFICIARIES OF QUALIFIED PENSION PLAN TO REVOCABLE TRUST

Plan _____

Action	Completed
1. Read the trust	
2. Review options with your advisors	
3. Write letter (9-4 or 9-5)	
4. Receive confirmation of change	

Life Insurance

As a practical matter, there is not a lot of benefit to be gained by transferring the ownership of your life insurance policy to your revocable living trust. There are many estate planning tactics that successfully use life insurance within irrevocable trusts. Life insurance within a revocable trust will still have the death benefits included in your estate for estate tax purposes.

The biggest advantage to placing your life insurance ownership in your trust would be to provide a successor trustee with authority to manage your policy in case you become incapacitated and are replaced as the trustee. It also gives your successor trustee more notice of the existence of your policy.

A more important consideration is whether to change either your primary or contingent beneficiary to your trust. Here, the most important aspect is how you wish to have the proceeds of your policy handled. If you want them to go directly to certain beneficiaries, it would be better to name the beneficiaries in the policy. They will receive their benefits directly, without probate or income tax. This method is usually faster than waiting for the trustee to apply for the benefits and then make a distribution.

On the other hand, you may want your successor trustee to maintain control of the benefits and manage the funds in accordance with the terms you have specified in the trust. Then it is best to name the trust as the beneficiary.

Do what best fits your plan. Remember, as trustmaker, you are the creator of your trust and it should be structured to meet your desires.

In this section, we will assume that you have decided to either transfer an existing policy to your trust, or change the beneficiary designation to your trust. The mechanics of changing the ownership and/or beneficiary of your life insurance policy are similar to the previous ownership/beneficiary changes. The major difference is that life insurance companies often require you to use their forms. You can start the process by either contacting your insurance agent to request the necessary forms, or by writing directly to the insurance company.

Don't request both an ownership change and beneficiary change at the same time, as it may confuse the insurance company. First change the beneficiary, then change the ownership.

Sample letters 9-6, 9-7, and 9-8 will help you make these changes.

Checklist 9-9
TRANSFER OWNERSHIP/BENEFICIARY OF LIFE INSURANCE POLICY TO REVOCABLE TRUST

Policy #_____ Company_____

Action	Completed
1. Read the trust	
2. Review with your advisors	
3. Write letter (9-6, 9-7, or 9-8)	
4. Receive endorsement of change	

Sample Letter 9-6
TRANSFER OWNERSHIP OF LIFE INSURANCE
TO REVOCABLE TRUST

John Smith
Your street address
City, state, zip code

Date letter written

ABC Life Insurance Company
Their address
Their city, state, zip code

Ref: Life insurance policy (number) on life of John Smith

Dear Sir/Madam:

I request that the ownership of the above-referenced life insurance policy be transferred to my trust. The owner is:

John Smith and Mary Smith, trustees
(Name of trust) dated (date of trust)
Trustee's address
Trustee's city, state, zip code

The taxpayer ID number of the trust is my social security number: 123-45-6789.

Enclosed are the following:

1. Form W-9 for trust
2. (Certified extract of trust) or (appropriate pages of trust)

(If premiums are still being paid:)

Please send all future premium notices to the new owner.

Sincerely,   Accepted:

_____   _____

John Smith   John Smith, trustee

_____   _____

Mary Smith   Mary Smith, trustee

Sample Letter 9-7
CHANGE PRIMARY BENEFICIARY OF LIFE INSURANCE
TO REVOCABLE TRUST

John Smith
Your street address
City, state, zip code

Date letter written

ABC Life Insurance Company
Their address
Their city, state, zip code

Ref: Life insurance policy (number) on life of John Smith

Dear Sir/Madam:

I request the beneficiary designation for the above-referenced life insurance policy be changed as follow:

Primary beneficiary: (Name of trust) dated (date of trust)
Taxpayer ID number: 123-45-6789
Contingent beneficiary: None

Sincerely,

_____

John Smith

Signature guarantees are not normally required for life insurance policies.

Sample Letter 9-8
CHANGE CONTINGENT BENEFICIARY OF LIFE INSURANCE TO REVOCABLE TRUST

John Smith
Your street address
City, state, zip code

Date letter written

ABC Life Insurance Company
Their address
Their city, state, zip code

Ref: Life insurance policy (number) on life of John Smith

Dear Sir/Madam:

I request the beneficiary designation for the above-referenced life insurance policy be changed as follows:

Primary beneficiary: List all primary beneficiaries — names, addresses, social security numbers, relationship to you, and percentage to each.

Contingent beneficiary: (Name of trust) dated (date of trust)

Taxpayer identification number: 123-45-6789

Sincerely,

John Smith

Annuities

You can use the same letters and checklists for annuities that you use for life insurance policies. You can transfer the ownership to the trust, change the beneficiary to the trust, or do both.

Before making changes to or transferring an annuity, review your policy with your financial advisor. Some annuity policies have guaranteed values upon the death of an annuitant and/or owner, as well as the waiver of surrender charges upon the death of an annuitant or owner. Since a trust does not die, your heirs could lose that benefit. Check the wording of your annuity policy and make sure that you understand any benefits you may be giving up with a transfer of ownership to your trust.

The Internal Revenue Code allows only "natural persons" to accrue earnings in an annuity on a tax-deferred basis. I have found that different annuity companies interpret this in different ways for trusts. Check this out with your tax advisor and the annuity company before transferring an annuity to a trust. Normally having a revocable trust as owner of the policy will not be a problem.

If you are married, you should consider naming your spouse rather than your revocable living trust as the primary beneficiary. A spouse can continue to defer taxes on an annuity's past and future increase in value, while a trust would have to report all past growth as taxable income upon receipt of the proceeds. This is similar to the earlier discussion on naming beneficiaries for IRA's and other pension-type plans.

Checklist 9-10
TRANSFER OWNERSHIP/BENEFICIARY OF ANNUITY TO REVOCABLE TRUST

Policy #_____ Company_____

Action	Completed
1. Read the trust	
2. Review policy with advisor	
3. Write letter (9-6, 9-7, or 9-8)	
4. Receive endorsement of change	

Bank Accounts

Transferring bank accounts is easy—you are essentially dealing with cash. Many advisors consider this unnecessary, especially if the account is a joint account with your spouse. Check with your advisor before making your decision.

You can take care of this transfer in a couple of different ways.

1. Visit your bank and have the transfer made directly.

2. Transfer cash by writing a check payable to your trust as "John Smith, trustee, (name of your trust)." Then open a new account with that check.

Certificates of Deposit

Your bank may not be quite as cooperative with your request to transfer title on certificates of deposit because there is a little more paperwork for them to do. They probably will go along with you as long as you are not withdrawing your funds.

You can handle this type of transfer using the same concept as other transfers. Banks usually have their own forms and signature cards. If your bank is local, you might make a visit and find out what they require to make a transfer. If not, use sample letter 9-9 to get the ball rolling.

Checklist 9-11
TRANSFER CERTIFICATE OF DEPOSIT TO REVOCABLE TRUST
Bank _____ Account #_____

Action	Completed
1. Read the trust	
2. Visit bank or send letter (9-9) to obtain forms	
3. Complete required bank forms	
4. Receive acknowledgment of transfer	

Sample Letter 9-9
TRANSFER CERTIFICATE OF DEPOSIT TO REVOCABLE TRUST

John Smith (as currently titled)
Mary Smith
Your street address
City, state, zip code

Date letter written

ABC Bank
Their address
Their city, state, zip code

Ref: Certificate of deposit, (account number) — (list all CD's for this bank on one letter)

Dear Sir/Madam:

I (we) request that you transfer ownership of the above-named certificate(s) of deposit to my (our) trust. Ownership should be listed as:

John Smith and Mary Smith, trustees
(Name of trust) dated (date of trust)
Trustee's address
Trustee's city, state, zip code

The taxpayer identification number of the trust remains as my social security number: 123-45-6789. Enclosed are the following:

1. Form W-9 for trust (signed by trustee)
2. (Certified extract of trust) or (appropriate pages of trust)

If any additional forms are required to complete this transfer, please send them to my (our) address above.

Sincerely,   Accepted:

_____   _____
John Smith   John Smith, trustee

_____   _____
Mary Smith   Mary Smith, trustee

* A Medallion signature guarantee is not required, since no securities are involved.

Untitled Assets

Many of the assets that you want to transfer to your trust may not have any legal registration of title. These could include such things as gold, stamps, coins, antiques, jewelry, and other personal property items. These assets are easy to transfer because no third parties are involved.

The simplest procedure is to make a list of the assets you are transferring. State that you are transferring them to the trust. This is often done by your attorney as part of the preparation of your trust. This statement will usually include a catch-all phrase transferring "all other assets not specially excluded" to your trust. You will often find this as an attachment to your trust documents.

All of these steps may seem like a lot of work, but they are necessary to properly transfer all the correct assets to your trust. The process will save your heirs a significant amount of time, effort, and money in the future. After spending hundreds or thousands of dollars and a great deal of time preparing your revocable living trust documents, don't lose the benefits that you paid for by neglecting this part of the process! The benefits greatly outweigh the effort.

CHAPTER 10

■ ■ ■ ■ ■ ■ ■ ■ ■

Managing Your Revocable Living Trust After the Death of the First Spouse

While both spouses are still living, the trustees of most revocable living trusts have to expend very little effort in maintaining their trusts. Their major responsibility is to make sure that all appropriate assets are titled in the name of the trust and that an accurate record of these assets is maintained.

After the death of the first spouse, the surviving spouse and/or successor trustee(s) now have a significantly greater level of responsibility. Depending upon the terms of the trust, the trustee's duties may include:

1. Dividing the assets into two or more trusts;

2. Probating a portion of the deceased spouse's estate;

3. Preparing and filing Internal Revenue Service Form 706, the estate tax return; plus appropriate state death tax returns;

4. Preparing and filing Internal Revenue Service Form 1041, fiduciary income tax return; and appropriate state income tax returns for the probate portion of the deceased spouse's estate;

5. Preparing and filing Internal Revenue Service Form 1041, fiduciary income tax return; and appropriate state income tax returns for any irrevocable trust(s) created by the death of the deceased spouse; and

6. Maintaining appropriate records of the probated estate and the irrevocable trust(s).

While these tasks are very significant and will take some time and effort, they need not be overwhelming. After you have finished reading this chapter, you will understand why they are necessary and know how to get them done. I do recommend that you rely on your advisors to make sure that you handle these tasks correctly.

You are now at one of the most critical stages in the life of your trust. If you don't do things properly here, the ultimate beneficiaries could lose the tax benefits of your trust that you paid for. You could also end up paying more income tax over the years than is necessary.

Follow the checklists and adapt the sample letters to take care of your transfers. It will be a lot easier than you think.

Read the Trust

As always, reading and understanding your trust is an essential first step. Never assume that your trust is a "standard" revocable living trust. There is no such thing.

We will concentrate on the two most common ways that these trusts are handled after the death of the first spouse.

Read the Will

When a revocable living trust is involved, you may think that a will is unnecessary. That is not true. The trust should be accompanied by a will for each of the trustmakers. Normally, the will is very simple and usually states that any assets that are not in the trust will be placed into the trust after the person's death. These wills are often called *pour-over wills,* since everything previously omitted from the trust is "poured" into the trust.

Don't assume the will is just a simple pour-over will. You may be surprised when you read it. There may be special instructions pertaining to specific assets that were intentionally left out of the trust. The trustmaker(s) may have wanted to have a portion of the estate probated in order to provide the statutory notice to any potential creditors. It is even possible that an executor will be named who is different from the successor trustee(s).

Two Types of Revocable Living Trusts for Married Couples

There are many variations in the way that revocable living trusts are structured. In this chapter we are concentrating on how to manage a revocable living trust created by a married couple. After the death of one spouse, the remaining trustee may have the option to either divide the trust into two or more trusts or maintain the trust as one entity. This allows the survivor to evaluate the assets in the trust to determine if the potential estate tax savings are worth the effort required to split the trust into separate trusts. The option to split the trust may have been omitted completely; this is the simplest form of a revocable living trust.

The other common structure is one that requires the original trust to be split into two or more trusts upon the death of the first spouse. This is usually done to reduce the decrease in the value of the estate due to the potential estate tax upon the death of the surviving spouse. There also may be other reasons, such as protecting a portion of the estate for the future benefit of a specific beneficiary without affecting the lifestyle of the surviving spouse. This often occurs when one or both of the spouses had a previous marriage.

Managing the Trust When All Assets Are Retained in One Trust

If the trust document directs that all assets remain in the original revocable trust, with the surviving spouse as trustee, it is very much like having all assets inherited by the surviving spouse. No probate is required. No special income tax returns are required.

The assets are re-registered using the surviving spouse's social security number. Unless indicated otherwise in the trust document, the surviving spouse may manage all the assets as he or she deems appropriate.

The flow chart for this type of revocable living trust would look like Figure 10-1. This flow chart is a simplified version—your trust may have different rules and requirements.

A variation of this situation is where a different trustee replaces the deceased spouse, either as a co-trustee or as the sole trustee. This most often happens when the surviving spouse is disabled or it was previously determined that he or she does not have the experience or knowledge to manage the trust assets.

Figure 10-1

| Are both spouses alive? | **Yes** → | All assets in trust are treated for tax purposes as if owned by both spouses directly. Trust is fully revocable. Both spouses are trustees. |

No ↓

| Is one spouse alive? | **Yes** → | All assets in trust are treated for tax purposes as if owned by the surviving spouse directly. Trust is fully revocable. Surviving spouse is trustee. |

No ↓

Trust is now irrevocable.
Named successor is now the trustee.
Trust has own tax reporting requirements.
Follow rules of the trust.

Maintaining all of the assets in one revocable trust normally occurs in estates that are valued below the amount that is allowable to pass on to the ultimate heirs without triggering the estate tax. See page 86 in Chapter 8 for these exemption amounts (determined by the year of death).

Despite the relative simplicity of this type of arrangement, certain tasks must be completed to properly utilize the trust. Checklist 10-1 provides general guidelines to do them properly. This checklist may look intimidating, but it is really a very straightforward and logical set of procedures recognizing the new status of the assets in the trust. It will ensure that income from investments are reported under the correct social security number and eliminate the possibility of the Internal Revenue Service imposing backup withholding of 31% on your earnings. Future sales and transfers will be much easier if the correct trustee is listed on all accounts. The surviving spouse will collect all benefits due him or her.

You should start off this procedure the same way that you started each task in the past. Read the trust. Make sure that you fully understand the rules of your trust.

The next step is also important: READ THE WILL. Normally, the will simply transfers to the trust all assets not already in the trust. But it could have different features. Make sure you are following both the will and the trust. Assets that are already in the trust are not affected by the will.

Preparing the list of assets will be an easy task if the list has been maintained as recommended earlier in the book. If you don't already have the list, you need to make sure that the list you develop is as complete as possible. Your investment advisor and tax professional will be able to help you with this. Tax returns will list all assets that have reportable income. If you discover other assets after completing your transfers, don't panic. Just complete the paperwork as you did with the other assets and add them to your list.

Checklist 10-1
REVOCABLE LIVING TRUST AFTER DEATH OF FIRST SPOUSE — NO SPLIT OF ASSETS

Action	Completed
1. Read the trust	
2. Read the will.	
3. Prepare list of all assets in estate/trust with values at date of death.	
a. Obtain appraisals of all real estate, valued as of date of death.	
b. Obtain values for stocks, bonds, mutual funds, and other investments at date of death.	
4. Retitle assets to reflect correct trustee: a. Home	
b. Other real estate	
c. Stock and bond "house" accounts	
d. Stock/bond certificates	
e. Mutual funds	
f. Limited partnerships	
g. Bank accounts	
h. Loans	
i. Life insurance	
j. Annuities	
k. Other assets	

Checklist 10-1 (continued)

Action	Completed
5. Collect all assets for which trust is beneficiary: a. Life insurance policies	
b. Annuities	
c. Pensions	
d. Profit-sharing plans	
e. 401(k)/403(b) plans	
f. Deferred compensation plans	
g. IRA's	
h. Keogh plans	
6. Transfer all appropriate retirement/annuity assets to surviving spouse's account: a. Pensions	
b. Profit-sharing plans	
c. 401(k)/403(b) plans	
d. Deferred compensation plans	
e. IRA's	
f. Keogh plans	
7. Notify: a. Accountant/tax preparer	
b. Financial advisor	
c. Attorney	
8. File Form 706 and state death tax forms, if necessary.	

Obtaining Values

The value of your assets as of the date of death of the deceased spouse is extremely important information. Not only do you need to know what you have to support your standard of living for the rest of your life, but there are important tax implications for this value.

If the total value of the trust/estate exceeds the exemption amount on page 86, you are required to file Form 706 (estate tax) with the IRS. You may also be required to file the appropriate death tax forms with your state and possibly other states if you own property or a business outside of your home state. These would have to be filed even if you will pay no estate tax because all of the assets are being passed on to your surviving spouse. Each state has its own filing requirements. Check with your tax advisor.

Another tax aspect is also important. Most assets will receive a "step-up" in tax cost basis as a result of the death of the first spouse. This means that taxable capital gains will be calculated based upon the value of an asset as of the date of death rather than the original cost. This could produce significant tax savings in the future if these assets are sold. Notable exceptions to this step-up are annuities, pension-type programs, IRA's, and Series EE savings bonds. If you are depreciating an asset, such as a rental or piece of business equipment, you will be able to start a new depreciation schedule using the current value and a full new lifetime.

■ Real Estate

One of the most neglected tasks in this area is obtaining the value of your home and other real estate. Since you can't just look up the value in a newspaper, procrastination often prevents this evaluation from being completed. The best way to do this is to have a qualified appraiser place a value on your property. This will give you a solid basis for reporting this value in the future. The disadvantage of an appraisal is the cost. It may be a few hundred dollars for your home or small residential rental property, and more expensive for land or commercial property. If the Internal Revenue Service should challenge this value in the future, the more professional the appraisal, the more likely it is that you will win.

A less expensive approach is to obtain a written estimate of value from a local real estate professional familiar with the type of real estate that you own. Most real estate agents are happy to give you such an estimate, as they would like the opportunity to list your property should you decide to sell in the future. While this type of evaluation is better than no evaluation, it does have its drawbacks. Many real estate agents, rightly so, are hesitant to put their estimates down on paper. Since their estimates are not full appraisals, they do not want to be held liable if the Internal Revenue Service attacks the value in the future. An IRS appraisal providing a different value would probably override an agent's estimate of value. Also, many agents will not commit to specific values, but instead will provide a range of value. This leaves you with having to set your own values within this range.

No matter which method you use to evaluate your real estate, do it as soon as possible. The longer you wait, the harder it will be to determine an accurate value as of the date of death. Too many times I have had clients try to determine these values many years after the fact. Save time and money by doing it now.

■ Stocks, Bonds, and Mutual Funds

Obtaining the value of listed stocks and mutual funds is a relatively simple process. These prices are published daily in the *Wall Street Journal* and many other newspapers around the country. When one of my clients passes away I file the appropriate *Wall Street Journal* listings for future use. The Internal Revenue Service requires that you use the average of the beginning and ending value on the day of death. The daily newspaper listings will provide you with—as a minimum—the closing price and the change from the previous close. You can use this information to determine the average price for both stocks and mutual funds. If the death occurred on a day that the stock market was closed (a weekend or holiday), you will use the average of the previous trading day and the next trading day. If all of your stocks are listed in your local paper, just save the appropriate issue or issues. If not, obtain a copy of the *Wall Street Journal* for the necessary days.

Not all securities are listed in the newspaper. Some stocks are traded "over the counter" and do not have daily listings. For these stocks, it will be necessary to contact your stockbroker or investment advisor to obtain data for the proper date. You may also be able to obtain this data from various Internet sites.

Some mutual funds are not reported in the newspapers. Occasionally, prices for listed funds are not available before the newspaper deadline for going to print. If this is the case, either have your investment advisor obtain these values or call the mutual fund directly.

Bonds generally are not listed in the newspapers. The primary reason is that each individual issue is generally not traded each day. Have your stockbroker or investment advisor obtain the correct quotes.

The use of an outside service such as Evaluation Services, Inc., 180 Old Tappan Road, Old Tappan, NJ 07675, (201) 784-8500, may prove helpful. They can provide historical values for stocks and bonds.

■ Limited Partnerships and Non-Traded Stocks

It is more difficult to obtain accurate valuations for limited partnerships and closely held (non-traded) stocks since there is usually very little trading actively. The best method is to contact the partnership or closely held corporation directly in order to obtain a reasonable value. Have them send this information to you in a letter, if possible. If they won't put it in writing, obtain as much information as you can concerning how they arrived at the value, and also make a note of the name and position of the individual who gives you the information. The more backup material you have, the more acceptable it will be to the IRS. For some partnerships and small corporations, it may be prudent to engage the services of a certified public accountant (CPA) who specializes in business evaluation to provide an accurate valuation.

■ Annuities/Pensions

You can obtain the value of your annuities in the same way that you determined the value of your non-listed mutual funds. Contact either your financial advisor or the life insurance company directly.

For pensions, 401(k)'s, and other types of deferred compensation plans, you should be able to obtain a value from the plan administrator.

■ Businesses

If an operating business is involved as an asset of your trust, you will probably need a CPA who specializes in business valuations to obtain a valid value for you.

I'm sure you can see the value of working with an investment professional. With one telephone call, you should be able to turn over most of the effort in valuing the investments in your trust, and you will know you are getting credible estimates if the IRS ever questions your calculations.

Retitling Assets

Even though you are not changing the trust after the death of the deceased spouse, you are making a change in the management of the trust and its assets. Whether you as the surviving spouse are now the sole trustee, or a successor co-trustee has been added, different signatures are now required to conduct the business of the trust.

The process for updating the names of the trustee(s) is very similar to the process that you used to originally transfer the assets into your trust. If you think about this process in that context, it will be simple and easy to understand.

■ Real Estate

Since there is no real change in ownership in this situation, there is no need to make any changes in your real estate titling at this time. If you sell your property at a future date, you will have to provide whoever does the title verification with a copy of the trust and a death certificate to prove that the correct trustee is making the sale.

■ Mutual Funds, Managed Accounts, Brokerage Accounts, Limited Partnerships

For most of the remaining assets, the retitling process will use letters very similar to the sample letters in Chapter 9 used to transfer assets into your trust. The concept is that you are notifying the transfer agent of the change in trustee status due to the death of one of the trustees. You are also supplying them with the necessary documentation to allow them to properly prepare future income and/or redemption checks, process a change of ownership if you sell, and report income and sales to the IRS.

In most cases the taxpayer ID number for the trust has been the husband's social security number. If the husband was the one who died, you will need to change the taxpayer ID number to the wife's social security number. You can do this with the same letter.

The sample letters that follow are formats that I have found to be effective in accomplishing this retitling. As with the other sample letters in this book, they should not be considered legal forms. Your attorneys or other advisors may use different letters that are just as effective.

Sample Letter 10-1
RETITLE MUTUAL FUNDS, MANAGED ACCOUNTS, BROKERAGE ACCOUNTS, AND LIMITED PARTNERSHIPS AFTER DEATH OF FIRST SPOUSE IN REVOCABLE LIVING TRUST

Name of trust
Your street address
City, state, zip code

Date letter written

(Mutual fund family, stock brokerage, etc.)
Their address
Their city, state, zip code

Ref: (Name of investment), (account number) — (could be more than one if in same mutual fund/limited partnership family)

Dear Sir/Madam:

I am the surviving trustee of the (name of the trust) dated (date of the trust). I request that the above-referenced account(s) be re-registered as follows:

> (Your name), trustee
> (Name of trust) dated (date of original trust)

The address will remain the same as the current registration. The taxpayer identification number will be my social security number: 123-45-6789.

Enclosed are the following:

1. Form W-9,
2. Certified copy of death certificate of (name of deceased spouse),
3. Notarized affidavit of domicile.

(For limited partnerships add this paragraph:)

I understand that since this is not a transfer of ownership and the retitling is due to the death of an owner, there are no transfer fees for this change.

Sincerely,

_____

(Your name), trustee

* Have signature Medallion-guaranteed.

Sample letter 10-1 provides all the documentation the company should need to complete the retitling. It includes the reason for the change and official notification by way of a death certificate. Be sure to send an original certified copy of the death certificate with the proper seal. A photocopy will not be acceptable to most transfer agencies.

The notarized affidavit of domicile will satisfy transfer agent attorneys that you are complying with all state laws concerning transfer after death. After using this form for several years, I have yet to determine exactly what it accomplishes other than if it isn't included, the paperwork is returned with a request for one. You can obtain these forms from most stock brokerages or financial planners. You can also make up your own form by copying the sample on page 137.

To meet the legal requirements, this form must be signed in front of a notary public who will acknowledge your signature.

The w-9 is the same form that you previously used when you first transferred these assets to your trust. It is simply a verification of your social security number. Without it, you could be subject to 31% tax withholding on all income and sale proceeds. You will find a Form w-9 in the appendix (page 238).

Limited partnerships usually impose a fee, generally in the range of $25 to $50, for transfer of ownership. I recommend that you add the last paragraph in letter 10-1 as an effort to avoid this fee. It doesn't always work, but it's sure worth the try.

It is possible that the transfer agent may require additional paperwork to complete the transfer. If they do, just follow their instructions.

Most securities transfer agents will also require that your request contain a signature guarantee from a member of the Medallion program. This is the same guarantee you needed when you transferred the assets into the trust.

AFFIDAVIT OF DOMICILE/NON-RESIDENT AFFIDAVIT/
AND DEBTS AFFIDAVIT

State of _____)
)ss.

County of _____)

_____ , being duly sworn, deposes and says that (she/he) resides at _____ , State of _____ and is (executor/administrator/surviving tenant) of the estate of _____ , deceased; who died at _____ on the _____ day of _____ , 19___ ; at the time of (his/her) death the domicile (legal residence) of said decedent was at _____ , County of _____ , State of _____ ; that decedent resided at such address for _____ years, such residence having commenced on _____ , 19___ ; that decedent last voted in the year of _____ at _____ , County of _____ , State of _____ ; that decedent's principal place of business at the time of (his/her) death was at _____ , County of _____ , State of _____ ; that decedent's most recent federal income tax return showed (his/her) legal residence as _____ , County of _____ , State of_____ ; that within three years prior to death decedent (was/was not) a resident of another state (if decedent resided in another state within three years prior to death, set forth the name of the state and facts as to change of residence and establishment of final domicile.)

That any and all debts, taxes, and claims against the estate have been paid or provided for; that this affidavit is made for the purpose of securing the transfer or delivery of property owned by decedent at the time of (his/her) death to a purchaser or the person or persons legally entitled thereto under the laws of decedent's domicile; and that any apparent inequality in distribution has been satisfied or provided for out of other assets in the estate.

_____
(executor/administrator/survivor)

Subscribed and sworn to (or affirmed) before me
this _____ day of _____ , 19 ___
by _____

_____
(Give official capacity of official administering oath.)

Just like the other aspects in taking care of your trust, these re-titlings do follow a logical pattern. Checklist 10-2 provides a guide for making these changes.

Checklist 10-2
RETITLE MUTUAL FUNDS, STOCK ACCOUNTS, MANAGED ACCOUNTS, AND LIMITED PARTNERSHIP IN REVOCABLE LIVING TRUST AFTER DEATH OF FIRST SPOUSE

Name of Asset _____

Action	Completed
1. Read the trust	
2. Write letter (10-1)	
3. Trustee sign (signature guaranteed)	
4. Mail letter	
5. Complete additional requirements	
6. Receive acknowledgment of completed transfer	

■ Individual Stock/Bond Certificates

The procedure for retitling individual stock and bond certificates parallels what you did when you initially transferred them into the trust. If you want to review these concepts, look back at Chapter 9.

Use sample letter 10-2 to complete the retitling of your stock and bond certificates. In addition to the signature guarantee on the letter, you should have your signature guaranteed on the stock certificate(s) or stock/bond power, whichever you choose to use.

Checklist 10-3 will guide you through this transfer process.

Sample Letter 10-2
RETITLE INDIVIDUAL STOCK AND BOND CERTIFICATES AFTER DEATH OF FIRST SPOUSE IN REVOCABLE LIVING TRUST — NO SPLIT OF TRUST

Name of trust
Your street address
City, state, zip code

Date letter written

Transfer agent
Their address
Their city, state, zip code

Ref: (Name of corporation), (CUSIP number), (number of shares), (certificate number(s))

Dear Sir/Madam:

I am the surviving trustee of the (name of trust) dated (date of the trust). I request that the above-referenced and enclosed certificate(s) be re-registered as follows:

(Your name), trustee
(Name of trust) dated (date of original trust)

The address will remain the same as the original registration. The taxpayer identification number will be my social security number: 123-45-6789.

In addition to the certificate, enclosed are the following:

1. Stock/bond powers (if used),
2. Form W-9,
3. Certified copy of death certificate of (name of deceased spouse), and
4. Notarized affidavit of domicile.

Sincerely,

_____

(Your name), trustee

* Have signature Medallion-guaranteed.

Checklist 10-3
RETITLE INDIVIDUAL STOCK/BOND CERTIFICATES IN REVOCABLE LIVING TRUST AFTER DEATH OF FIRST SPOUSE — NO SPLIT OF TRUST

Name of Stock/Bond _____

Action	Completed
1. Read the trust	
2. Locate certificate/bond	
3. Determine transfer agent and address	
4. Write letter (10-2)	
5. Trustee sign (signature guaranteed)	
6. Sign stock certificate/bond/stock power (signature guaranteed)	
7. Mail letter by registered, insured U.S. Mail	
8. Receive new certificate in name of trust	
9. Photocopy certificate	
10. Trustee safely store certificate	

If you have misplaced your stock or bond certificate, follow the same procedures outlined in Chapter 9 to replace the lost certificates. Use sample letter 10-3 to initiate the process.

After making the effort required to transfer individual stock/bond certificates, even if you haven't misplaced them, I think you will agree that it may be easier and more efficient to maintain these certificates in a brokerage account with your financial planner or stockbroker. Once you have received your new certificate, this can be done with very little effort.

Sample Letter 10-3
RETITLE AND REISSUE LOST STOCK/BOND CERTIFICATE IN REVOCABLE LIVING TRUST AFTER DEATH OF FIRST SPOUSE — NO SPLIT OF TRUST

Name of trust
Your street address
City, state, zip code

Date letter written

Transfer agent
Their address
Their city, state, zip code

Ref: (Name of corporation), (CUSIP number if known), (number of shares if known), (certificate number if known)

Dear Sir/Madam:

I am the surviving trustee of the (name of trust) dated (date of trust). The trust is the owner of (number of shares if known) shares in the above-referenced company. I am unable to locate these shares.

I request that these shares be re-issued and re-registered as follows:

(Your name), trustee
(Name of trust), dated (date of original trust)

The address will remain the same as the original registration. The taxpayer identification number will be my social security number: 123-45-6789.

Enclosed are the following:

1. Form W-9,
2. Certified copy of death certificate of (name of deceased spouse),
3. Notarized affidavit of domicile.

I understand that you may require additional forms and a surety bond to complete this transfer. Please forward your requirements to my address above.

Sincerely,

_____
(Your name), trustee

* Have signature Medallion-guaranteed.

Checklist 10-4
RETITLE LOST STOCK/BOND CERTIFICATE IN REVOCABLE LIVING TRUST AFTER DEATH OF FIRST SPOUSE — NO SPLIT OF TRUST

Name of Stock/Bond _____

Action	Completed
1. Read the trust	
2. Determine number of shares owned	
3. Determine transfer agent and address	
4. Write letter (10-3)	
5. Trustee sign (signature guaranteed)	
6. Mail letter	
7. Receive instructions/forms from transfer agent	
8. Return required letters with check for bond to transfer agent	
9. Receive new certificates in name of trust	
10. Photocopy certificate	
11. Store certificate	

■ Annuities

Annuities are a hybrid asset. They are a combination of an investment and a life insurance policy. They are also a contract between the owner of the annuity and the insurance company.

Throughout the book I have been reminding you to read the trust. Now it is important to read the annuity. Your action with the annuity will depend upon the terms of the annuity contract.

You must first determine the owner of the annuity, the annuitant, and the beneficiary. You may find that the annuity contract also specifies successor owner(s), contingent annuitants, and contingent beneficiaries.

The annuitant could be the deceased spouse, the surviving spouse, both spouses as joint annuitants, or another named individual. The owner could be the trust, the deceased spouse, or the surviving spouse; or there could be joint ownership by both spouses. The beneficiary could be either the spouse, the trust, or someone else.

Once you know who all of the participants are, you must determine what the annuity specifies will occur upon the death of the spouse who died. Then you can proceed with the proper steps.

The action requiring distribution of the annuity and/or its assets is usually the death of the owner or the annuitant. Contracts are written both ways.

There is one area in which the life insurance companies that issue the annuities are consistent. They all require their own forms in order to make changes to a policy or obtain death claims. Contact the insurance agent or financial advisor who set up the annuity. Inform them of the situation and ask for the appropriate forms. As an alternative, you can call the insurance company directly.

Checklist 10-5
PROCESS ANNUITY POLICY IN REVOCABLE LIVING
TRUST UPON DEATH OF FIRST SPOUSE

Insurance Company _____
Policy Number _____

Action	Completed
1. Read the trust	
2. Read the policy	
a. Determine function of deceased spouse	
b. Determine change required	
3. Contact advisor/insurance company	
4. Receive forms from insurance company	
5. Return completed forms to insurance company	
6. Receive confirmation of change and annuity proceeds	

■ Life Insurance

Life insurance, like annuities, involves a contract with three parties in addition to the insurance company: the owner, the insured, and the beneficiary. The trust could be the owner, the beneficiary, or both. Be sure to read the policy to determine this.

If the deceased spouse is the insured and the trust is the beneficiary, the trustee must obtain the proceeds of the policy for the trust. Just like the annuity, the insurance company will require its own forms. The easiest way to take care of this is to contact the life insurance agent or financial planner who set up the policy and have them obtain the necessary forms. You can also call the insurance company directly.

If there are other beneficiaries in addition to the trust, make sure that you receive the proper number of forms from the life insurance company. They often want one claim form per beneficiary. You will need to provide them with a certified copy of the death certificate.

Make a copy of the life insurance policy before you mail it. This is a safety factor in case the policy becomes lost in the mail.

Checklist 10-6 is a guide to the process of obtaining the death benefits for the trust.

Checklist 10-6
REVOCABLE LIVING TRUST IS BENEFICIARY OF LIFE INSURANCE DEATH BENEFITS UPON THE DEATH OF FIRST SPOUSE

Insurance Company _____
Policy Number _____

Action	Completed
1. Read the trust	
2. Read the policy	
3. Contact advisor/life insurance company	
4. Receive forms from life insurance company	
5. Copy policy before mailing to life insurance company	
6. Return completed form to life insurance company	
7. Receive death benefit proceeds	

If the trust was listed as the owner of the policy and the policy is insuring the surviving spouse, you will have to notify the life insurance company of the change in the named trustee. Use sample letter 10-4 and checklist 10-7 to complete this task.

Sample Letter 10-4
NOTIFY LIFE INSURANCE COMPANY OF CHANGE OF TRUSTEE FOR INSURANCE POLICY ON LIFE OF SURVIVING TRUSTEE UPON DEATH OF FIRST SPOUSE WHERE OWNER OF POLICY IS REVOCABLE LIVING TRUST WITH NO SPLIT OF ASSETS

Name of trust
Your street address
City, state, zip code

Date letter written

ABC Life Insurance Company
Their address
Their city, state, zip code

Ref: Life insurance policy number (_____) on life of
(surviving spouse)

Dear Sir/Madam:

I am the (surviving) (successor) trustee of the (name of trust) dated (date of trust). The previous (co-)trustee, (name of deceased spouse), died on (date of death). Please change your record of ownership of the above-referenced policy to read:

(Name of trustee)
(Name of trust) dated (date of trust)
Trustee's address
Trustee's city, state, zip code

The taxpayer identification number of the trust is my social security number: 123-45-6789.

Enclosed are the following:

1. Form W-9
2. Copy of death certificate of (named of deceased spouse).

(If premiums are still being paid:)

Please send all future premium notices to the trust at the above address.

Sincerely,

_____
(Your name), trustee

If the life insurance policy is designed to provide death benefits only after the death of both spouses, commonly called a *last-to-die policy,* you would use a letter similar to letter 10-4. Change the reference line to read:

Ref: Life insurance policy number (_____) on the lives of (_____) and (_____)

Checklist 10-7
NOTIFY LIFE INSURANCE COMPANY OF CHANGE OF TRUSTEE
FOR INSURANCE POLICY UPON DEATH OF FIRST SPOUSE
WHEN POLICY OWNER IS REVOCABLE LIVING TRUST

Insurance Company _____

Policy Number _____

Action	Completed
1. Read the trust	
2. Read the policy	
3. Write letter (10-4)	
4. Receive acknowledgment of change from insurance company	

■ IRA's, Pensions, and Other Qualified Tax Deferral Plans

These plans would not be owned by the revocable living trust. The trust will probably not be the beneficiary of these plans due to adverse tax consequences. The most likely situation is that the surviving spouse will be the beneficiary of any plans owned by the deceased spouse. It is also possible that other beneficiaries may have been named.

Even though the trustee and the trust are usually not involved with these retirement plans, the surviving spouse usually will be receiving the benefits. Many plans have already been set up by contract to provide a specified monthly income for the surviving spouse. Others will give the survivor several options such as a lump sum, a rollover to the survivor's IRA, or monthly income.

Contact the plan administrator to find out your options and request the appropriate beneficiary forms. Review these options with your advisors to determine the best one for your particular situation. In making your decision, consider the following:

1. Your living expenses,
2. Your health,
3. Your other sources of income,
4. Other assets that can produce income,
5. Effects of future inflation, and
6. What you want to do with your money.

Checklist 10-8
DISBURSEMENT OF IRA'S, PENSIONS, AND OTHER QUALIFIED TAX DEFERRAL PLANS AFTER DEATH OF OWNER (FIRST SPOUSE TO DIE)
Name of Plan_____

Action	Completed
1. Review plan	
2. Contact plan administrator/IRA custodian for options and forms	
3. Consult with advisor	
4. Submit proper forms	
5. Collect benefits	

■ Other Death Benefits

Many employers, labor unions, military benefit plans, and pensions provide lump sum death benefits in addition to the pension plans that we discussed. Sometimes you have to do a little detective work to find out if any are available. Normally the trust will not be involved unless it was named as the beneficiary.

Check with the deceased spouse's employer, labor union, and/or pension to see if there is a death benefit. If so, request that the appropriate forms be sent to you.

Another area to check is social security. If the deceased spouse was eligible for social security, the surviving spouse may be eligible for a $255 social security "burial benefit." Surviving spouses over the age of 60, or dependent children under age 18, may also be eligible for monthly income benefits. Contact your local social security office for details.

Checklist 10-9
OTHER POTENTIAL DEATH BENEFITS
FOR SURVIVING SPOUSE

Action	Completed
1. Check with employer	
2. Check with union	
3. Check with social security office	
4. Check with pension	

■ Bank Accounts and Certificates of Deposit

Retitling accounts with your bank should be an easy matter. Just like with mutual funds and other investments, you are simply changing the name of the trustee on the account and possibly changing the social security number. You will probably keep the same account number, but some banks will want to set up a new account.

If the bank is local, it is probably easiest to visit with them and take care of the changes in person. If you prefer, you may use sample letter 10-5 to take care of this by mail.

Checklist 10-10
RETITLE BANK ACCOUNTS UPON DEATH OF FIRST
SPOUSE FOR REVOCABLE LIVING TRUST

Action	Completed
1. Read the trust	
2. Make list of all bank accounts	
3. Visit bank or write letter (10-5)	
4. Receive notification of change	

■ **Personal Property**

This is the easiest part of your job. Since most personal property is not registered in your name or the trust's name, there is nothing that needs to be done for these items. Take a little extra time to make a list of any significant items that you own. You may also want to consider specifying any assets that you desire to go to specific heirs after your death. This will give your successor trustee helpful guidance.

The ownership of an automobile is normally registered with your state. Many attorneys and advisors recommend that you have them registered in your trust's name. Others feel that it is not necessary. It usually requires a simple form from your Department of Motor Vehicles.

Sample Letter 10-5
RETITLE BANK ACCOUNTS UPON DEATH OF FIRST
SPOUSE FOR REVOCABLE LIVING TRUST

Name of trust
Your street address
City, state, zip code

Date letter written

ABC Bank
Their address
Their city, state, zip code

Ref: Account numbers _____

Dear Sir/Madam:

I am the (surviving trustee [or] successor trustee) of the (name of trust) dated (date of trust). The previous (co-)trustee, (name of deceased spouse), died on (date of death). Please change the title of ownership for the above-referenced accounts to read:

(Name of trustee)
(Name of trust) dated (date of trust)
Trustee's address
Trustee's city, state, zip code

The taxpayer identification number of the trust is my social security number: 123-45-6789.

Enclosed are the following:

1. Form W-9
2. Copy of death certificate (name of deceased spouse).

If any additional forms are required, please send them to my address above.

Sincerely,

_____

(Your name), trustee

Revocable Living Trust With Assets Split Into Two Or More Trusts Upon First Death

The second general type of revocable living trust is one in which the assets are split into two or more trusts upon the death of the first spouse. As mentioned earlier in this chapter, the purpose of creating these additional trusts is usually to eliminate or reduce estate taxes on the overall estate.

The common A/B trust will be used to explain how the trust assets should be managed after the death of the first spouse. The same considerations and sample letters can be used with slight modifications if a more complex trust has been created by the trustmakers.

Figure 10-2 is a flow chart for an example of an A/B type of revocable living trust. Do not assume that your trust will follow this exact pattern. There are as many variations as there are different attorneys, individual needs, and situations.

Trust A in Figure 10-2 is set up to manage the surviving spouse's separate property and his or her share of joint and community property. It can be called various names by the trustmakers, such as *survivor's trust, marital trust, exclusion trust, marital trust 1, Trust A,* or any other name. I have even seen it called *Trust B.* The name is immaterial. What is important is how it is handled. For purposes of simplicity, I will use the term Trust A.

For estate tax purposes, all assets assigned to this trust are assumed inherited and owned by the surviving spouse. These assets are not subject to the estate tax since transfer between spouses is 100% excluded from taxation.

Trust A is normally still a revocable trust. The surviving spouse has the right to manage the assets as he or she wishes. Assets may be sold, given away, or consumed as desired. They can be removed from the trust and the trust can be changed or completely revoked if so directed by the surviving spouse.

Since the trust is revocable by the trustmaker, with the surviving trustmaker acting as trustee and receiving all of the benefits, no fiduciary income tax return (Form 1041) is required. All income and deductions are reported directly on the surviving spouse's regular income tax return (Form 1040).

Figure 10-2

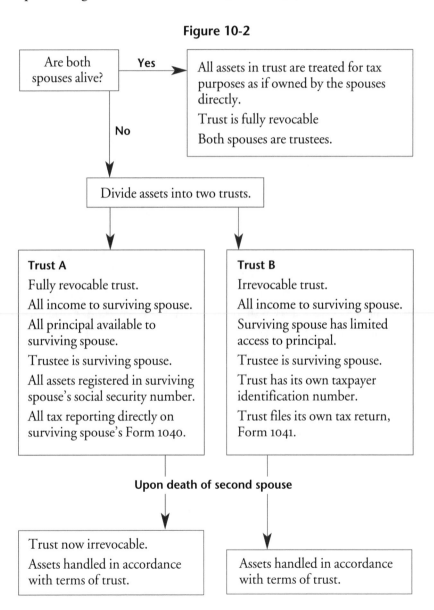

Trust B in the diagram is a completely different entity. It also may be called by various names, such as *bypass trust, exemption trust, marital trust 2, credit shelter trust,* or any other name as designated in the trust document. I will call it Trust B.

Assets are placed in Trust B according to the terms of the trust. The trust may require that 50% of the assets be placed in Trust B. Often a maximum amount is listed, equal to the amount that can be excluded from estate taxation due to the unused amount of the unified credit that is available. This credit is equivalent to the taxable transfer of between $625,000 and $1,000,000 (depending on the year of death) less any amount previously used and reported on a gift tax return. Other amounts may also be used. Be sure to read the trust to determine the correct amount.

The purpose of Trust B is usually to take maximum advantage of the unified credit that is available to the deceased spouse's estate. In order to prevent these assets from being taxed in the surviving spouse's estate, they must be removed from the survivor's estate. This is accomplished by making Trust B an irrevocable trust. Now you have a completely separate legal entity. As an irrevocable trust, Trust B will have its own taxpayer identification number and will file a fiduciary income tax return (Form 1041). See Chapter 7 for tax details.

The surviving spouse usually receives all of the income from Trust B and may be authorized by the trust document, within limitations, to remove principal after Trust A has been consumed. If the income is received by the surviving spouse, he or she will pay tax on the income. Normally, capital gains are not considered income, but are retained in the trust as part of the principal. Reading the trust document will tell you how to handle this.

Trust B cannot make charitable contributions unless specifically authorized by the trust document.

It is the fiduciary duty of the trustee of Trust B to manage the trust, following all rules written in the trust, for the benefit of the current income beneficiary (usually the surviving spouse) and also for the benefit of the ultimate contingent beneficiaries.

Now that you understand the differences between Trusts A and B, it's time to get into action. Checklist 10-11 will guide you through the process. It is similar to checklist 10-1, but a few extra steps are necessary.

The first two extra steps are fairly simple. Since Trust B is a separate reporting and paying entity, you must obtain a taxpayer identification number for it. This will be necessary for income reporting purposes and for retitling assets into Trust B. If additional trusts are involved, a separate taxpayer ID number is needed for each trust. Trust A will use the surviving spouse's social security number. Use Internal Revenue Service Form SS-4 to obtain the taxpayer ID number. You can find a copy in the appendix (page 236). If your advisor doesn't have a blank form available you can call the Internal Revenue Service Forms Line toll-free at 1-800-829-3676 and they will send you one.

You will also have to file a second form with the IRS notifying them of your fiduciary capacity as trustee of Trust B. Use Form 56 for this purpose. You can find a copy in the appendix (page 237) or request a blank form from the Internal Revenue Service at the same time you order Form SS-4. Be sure to attach a copy of the trust document as required on the form.

The third extra step is the most important: splitting the trust into the separate subtrusts.

Some attorneys and other vendors of trusts will state that an actual split of the assets and retitling them in the names of the two trusts is not necessary. I don't believe them. The accounting problem in all but the simplest of cases would be a nightmare. Without truly separating the assets into the required different trusts, it would be difficult, if not impossible, to convince the IRS at a later date that they were truly separate entities. Do your job right and make it easy on yourself.

Checklist 10-11
REVOCABLE LIVING TRUST AFTER DEATH OF FIRST SPOUSE WITH SPLIT OF ASSETS

Action	Completed
1. Read the trust	
2. Read the will	
3. Obtain taxpayer ID number for Trust B (Form ss-4)	
4. File Form 56 with IRS	
5. Prepare list of all assets in estate/trust with values at date of death.	
a. Obtain appraisals for all real estate, valued as of date of death.	
b. Obtain values for stocks, bonds, and mutual funds at date of death (retain copy of *Wall Street Journal* for following day).	
6. Determine split of assets among A/B and any other trusts.	
7. Retitle assets to appropriate trusts: a. Home	
b. Other real estate	
c. Stock and bond "house" accounts	
d. Stock certificates	
e. Mutual funds	
f. Limited partnerships	
g. Bank accounts	
h. Loans	
i. Life insurance	

Checklist 10-11 (continued)

Action	Completed
j. Annuities	
k. Other assets	
8. Collect all assets for which trust is beneficiary: a. Life insurance policies	
b. Annuities	
c. Pensions	
d. Profit-sharing plans	
e. 401(k) plans	
f. Deferred compensation plans	
g. IRA's	
h. Keogh plans	
9. Transfer all retirement/annuity assets as appropriate to surviving spouse's account: a. Pensions	
b. Profit-sharing plans	
c. 401(k) plans	
d. Deferred compensation plans	
e. IRA's	
f. Keogh plans	
10. Notify: a. Accountant/tax preparer	
b. Financial advisor	
c. Attorney	

Splitting the Assets Between the Trusts

The time has come to make the actual division of assets. Your decisions will have long-term implications for both the surviving spouse and the ultimate beneficiaries. The division will affect income, taxes, and the final amount inherited after the death of the second spouse.

What makes this division interesting is that there are no hard and fast rules for you to follow. You must read and interpret the trust document to determine what the trustmakers actually wanted when they set up the trust. Then you must position the assets to meet these goals. I recommend that you consult with advisors who:

1. Understand your situation and your needs,

2. Understand the investments involved, and

3. Understand the tax implications of the options.

Except in the simplest of situations, the splitting of assets is not a do-it-yourself proposition. Use professional advisors to help you.

"Honey, tell me one last time, is mine the A trust or the B trust?"

There are two ways to approach the division of assets. One concept is that each asset should be divided evenly between the two trusts. This may be a fair way to approach the problem, but it is not very flexible or practical. There are some attorneys who feel that the tax laws require it be done this way. This is a matter of opinion; there have been no definite rulings to support their position.

The second method is to divide the assets in such a manner as to provide the dollar amount required for each trust by the trust agreement. This way you can divide the assets based upon the most beneficial allocation to meet the needs of the beneficiaries.

The allocation of the assets between the trusts will be determined by the language of the trust. The division by dollar amount is preferred by most advisors, as it generally is the easiest and gives the best results. Our discussion will be based upon this method.

Considerations in Placing Assets in Trusts A and B

■ *Income Requirements of Surviving Spouse*

Absolutely the most important consideration when splitting assets among the trusts is to provide for the income needs of the surviving spouse. Always make sure that he or she is adequately provided with the means to maintain his or her desired lifestyle, if possible. This supersedes any considerations of tax consequences or inheritances by the ultimate beneficiaries.

Your planning here will probably be influenced by the fact that most revocable living trusts prepared for a husband and wife require that all income from both the trusts (for example, Trust A and Trust B) be distributed to the surviving spouse each year.

The trustee usually has the right and the responsibility to meet the goals of the trust. This could include selling assets and replacing them with more appropriate assets if need be.

Another income consideration is that not all positive cash flow is classified as income. Real estate rentals or equipment leasing investments may produce a positive cash flow that is sheltered by depreciation. A portion of income from oil or gas wells is partially sheltered by depletion. The trustee must evaluate the need for cash flow in determining where to place these assets. If there is no need for this cash flow, Trust B may be a good place to provide for retention and build-up of assets. If there is a need for the cash flow, Trust A may be a better choice.

■ Tax Considerations

There are several tax aspects to consider when determining the split of assets. The trustee must determine which assets are the most important for the particular situation of the trust.

Trust B is a separate tax reporting entity. Review Chapter 7 for the tax rules. Any undistributed income is likely to be taxed at the higher fiduciary tax rate (rather than the surviving spouse's tax rate). This may have little or no bearing on your decisions if all income is actually distributed. It may have a major impact if some of the income is not distributed.

While most trusts do require the distribution of income, they do not provide for the distribution of capital gains. This is logical since capital gains are really part of the principal of the trust. For example, if you sell a parcel of land, the total value of the trust will be exactly the same after the sale as before the sale. You have just exchanged one asset (the land) for another (cash). There is no income. This means that capital gains normally will be taxed to the trust. Fortunately, trusts have the same maximum federal capital gains rates as individuals. There is usually no major difference in the capital gains tax amount, regardless of whether the trust or the surviving spouse pays it, unless the surviving spouse is in the 15% tax bracket.

One thing to watch out for is the capital gains distributions from mutual funds. Long-term capital gains are no problem since you handle them the same for both individual returns and fiduciary returns. Short-term capital gains are different. Mutual funds include short-term capital gains as part of the "ordinary dividends" on Form 1099-DIV. This is because they are taxed at the same rates as ordinary income, not the lower capital gains rates. This causes no problems on an individual's Form 1040. However, on a trust's Form 1041, these short-term capital gains must be treated as capital gains (but should not be distributed as income unless the trust document allows for it). Normally these short-term gains will be taxed at ordinary income rates, unless balanced with capital losses.

The only way to determine if the ordinary dividend section of your mutual fund Form 1099-DIV contains short-term capital gains is to look at your mutual fund statements that you received when the dividends were credited to the account. You will often see entries identifying dividends or either "income," "short-term gains," or "long-term gains."

The most significant reason for splitting the assets into two trusts is to remove the assets placed in Trust B from the surviving spouse's estate. Once in Trust B, these assets will not be subject to estate tax upon the death of the surviving spouse. This is because the trust does not die, but continues to operate under the terms of the trust document until finally distributed to the final beneficiaries. This is true no matter what value these assets may have grown to. This feature should cause you to consider placing assets with a potential for growth into Trust B in order to provide the maximum value to the beneficiaries upon the second death.

The estate-tax-free growth in Trust B does come with a balancing income tax cost. The income tax basis rules state that when you inherit property, you receive it with a tax cost basis equal to the value of the property at the date of death of the previous owner. For assets that appreciate in value (such as stocks and real estate), this step-up in basis can be a significant income tax benefit. The tax on all past appreciation is forgiven and the new owner has a fresh start.

Upon the second death there is no step-up in tax basis for the assets in Trust B beyond the original step-up upon the first spouse's death. There was no death of the owner of the assets since Trust B did not die. The income tax cost basis remains the same as it was upon the death of the first spouse. Any taxable gain or loss on future sales is based upon this earlier value.

This capital gains tax should not deter you from placing growth assets in Trust B. Capital gains taxes are lower than estate taxes. The maximum capital gains tax is 20% for most assets. The exceptions are recaptured real estate depreciation (taxed at 25%) and collectibles (taxed at 28%). All of these rates are less than the estate tax rate, which starts at 37% (or 39% starting in 2004, when the exclusion amount increases to $850,000).

The placement of the *primary residence* has some interesting tax implications. Current tax laws provide for a different treatment of the sale of a principal residence than it does for other assets. If the home has been used as the primary residence for two of the last five years, an individual is allowed to exclude from income up to $250,000 of gain when it is sold. The exclusion is $500,000 for a married couple. No loss is deductible if there is a loss.

Combined with the step-up in basis on the death of the first spouse, the surviving spouse will probably be able to sell the home in the foreseeable future without worrying about paying any capital gains tax if the home is placed in Trust A. If the surviving spouse plans to sell the home relatively soon after the first spouse's death there may even be a loss due to the expenses of selling the home (escrow costs, real estate brokerage fees, and other closing costs). This loss is not a deductible loss for the surviving spouse in Trust A.

If the home is placed in Trust B, any sale will be treated completely differently. The home will have the benefit of the step-up in basis due to the death of the first spouse. Trust B will not be able to claim the $250,000 exclusion for the sale of a personal residence. Trust B is an artificial legal entity and does not have a residence. Any gain will be taxed as a capital gain in the same manner as any other investment.

There is a plus side to this treatment of the sale of residence as a capital gain. If there is a loss, either due to closing costs or a drop in the home's value, Trust B will be able to use this loss to balance out any capital gains. Any unused capital losses will be passed on to the ultimate beneficiaries when Trust B is eventually closed down.

As you can see, there are no hard and fast rules to follow when placing the family residence in the trusts. If the surviving spouse plans to stay in the home for a significant length of time, it is a good idea to consider placing it in Trust A. If the home will be sold in the near future, consider Trust B. There also may be other overriding considerations.

There is one more tax aspect to consider. As you will recall, most B trusts require that all income be provided to the surviving spouses. You have until 65 days after the end of the year to determine the amount of income and distribute it.

A problem may arise if you place limited partnership interests within Trust B. Many partnerships are unable to provide the tax reporting information, in the form of Schedule K-1, to their partners in time to meet this 65-day deadline. Some do not complete this task until April 1 or later. If you place limited partnership interests within Trust B, you may be unable to calculate the amount of earning for the year for the trust. If you cannot calculate the earnings, you will be unable to distribute the proper amount of income to the surviving spouse in time. Take this potential problem into consideration when making your asset split decision. It could save you many headaches as well as a lot of money in the future.

If the surviving spouse doesn't have a need for income from Trust B, many trustees consider using annuities as part of the trust. There is some controversy as to the appropriateness of these annuities within an irrevocable trust such as Trust B. The Internal Revenue Code states that the income from annuities is not taxed if it is for the benefit of a "natural person."

Some legal departments of life insurance companies will consider Trust B a natural person as long as the annuitant and/or beneficiaries are natural persons. They will not report the income to the IRS. Others interpret the law literally and consider annuities owned by an irrevocable trust to be taxable income. Check with your insurance company before placing an annuity into a B trust.

The income issue may not be a problem with variable annuities. Variable annuities have many of the characteristics of a mutual fund, but all gain is deferred until the funds are removed from the annuity. Since a variable annuity is not required to pay reportable dividends, most variable annuities do not pay income and capital gains dividends. Instead, they will account for the total growth simply by adjusting the value per unit of the annuity account.

One problem with a variable annuity is you may lose one of the benefits that come with the investment. Most variable annuity policies contain a small life insurance policy that guarantees your heirs a certain minimum value in the account when you die, no matter what the fluctuations in stock market have done to value of your account. This guarantee may not be applicable to Trust B since a trust does not die. Check the terms of the policy. Some will pay the guarantee on the death of the owner, some on the annuitant.

Needs and Desires of the Ultimate Beneficiaries

You also want to consider the people who will eventually receive the benefits of the trusts. While their needs should be secondary to the needs of the surviving spouse, they may influence how you split the assets among the trusts.

This may have very little impact if the ultimate beneficiaries of both trusts are the same. If the beneficiaries of the trusts are different, it could be a major consideration as to where each asset is placed.

Some areas to think about here include sentimental values, which heirs could benefit the most from business ownership, who might eventually want to own the family residence or vacation home, and how the different heirs would be able to work together with jointly owned property in the future.

Life Insurance Within Trust B

Here is an alternative that you may want to consider if the surviving spouse has sufficient income. Use some of the assets in Trust B to purchase a life insurance policy on the surviving spouse. The best way is with a single premium policy.

You have the option of investing in a fixed, guaranteed cash value policy or a variable policy where the cash is invested in separate accounts similar to mutual funds. Either way the growth will not be subject to income tax during the holding period (unless Congress changes its mind about taxing life insurance cash value build-up). This will help solve the income tax reporting and liability problems for both the surviving spouse and the trust.

Upon the death of the surviving spouse, the face amount of the policy is available for disbursement by the trust on both an income-tax-free and estate-tax-free basis.

This concept provides the heirs with a guarantee of growth in the trust (the insurance death benefit must be more than the cash value) without concern about eventual capital gains or ordinary income taxes on the gains.

If you miscalculated and find out at a future date that more income is needed for the surviving spouse, life insurance can provide this. The cash value can either be withdrawn or borrowed from the policy. Taxes would have to be paid on this cash flow,

Figure 10-3
DETERMINING THE ASSET SPLIT

The Smith Family Trust Asset Split

Asset	Number of units	Price per unit	Total value
Real Estate			
Home (your street address)	1	$250,000.00	$250,000.00
Cabin in the Woods	1	$150,000.00	$150,000.00
Cash			
Checking, Our Bank			$1,500.50
Cert. of Deposit, Our Bank			$14,837.50
Accrued Interest			$15.85
Money Market Fund	11,543.14	$1.00	$11,543.14
Investments			
Mutual Fund XYX	4,412.155	$10.00	$44,121.55
Mutual Fund MNO	15,627.82	$20.00	$312,556.48
Stock ABC Corp.	3000	$25.00	$75,000.00
Real Estate Limited Partnership	20	$1,000.00	$20,000.00
Annuity, A Life Co.			$75,424.98
Personal Property			
Autos			$20,000.00
Jewelry			$10,000.00
Personal Effects			$15,000.00
Totals			$1,000,000.00

Figure 10-3 (continued)

The Smith Family Trust Asset Split

Trust A	Trust B	Account number	Address
$250,000.00			
	$150,000.00		
$1,500.50		1-34538	135 Main, Here, CA 95888
$14,837.50		2-34578	135 Main, Here, CA 95888
$15.85			
$11,543.14		101-5735	14 West, Atlanta, GA 30050
	$44,121.55	95-48723	976 South, Boston, MA 11111
$81,678.03	$230,878.45	55555	45 North, Dallas, TX 78888
	$75,000.00	XX-4226	111 East, West, OR 98887
$20,000.00		5478	497 West, Chicago, IL 67890
$75,424.98		1245678	95 Center, Omaha, NE 57891
$20,000.00			
$10,000.00			
$15,000.00			
$500,000.00	$500,000.00		

since Congress has decided that borrowing and withdrawing funds from life insurance policies where the premium was paid at a pace faster than normal (usually all at once) is a taxable event. This is not really a problem since most other sources of income are also taxed when received from Trust B.

Do not go into this option without fully understanding all the facts. Make sure that it fits the needs of all parties concerned. Shop around for the best policy. Use a competent and experienced life insurance agent who can guide you through the complexities of your many choices of policies. This is not a do-it-yourself program.

Take your time when deciding how to split the assets after the death of the first spouse. Consult your advisors and carefully consider all aspects of this decision.

As you work through the maze of this split, you may want to use a spreadsheet similar to Figure 10-3. This spreadsheet is very useful, not only in determining the proper split, but also in organizing all of the assets involved. You can prepare this spreadsheet on a sheet of paper, but you might find it easier to use a computer spreadsheet program such as Excel or Lotus 1-2-3.

Start by listing all of the assets in the first column. It is useful to include account numbers and addresses where appropriate to make it easier once you start writing letters to make the transfers. This will also make it easier to ensure that you have all the assets, both for this exercise and in case you have to file an estate tax return.

You can start this before you have all of the information. It will help you determine which items you still need to find, such as the number of shares and/or their value, in order to complete the task.

If you use a computer spreadsheet, you will be able to keep a running total of the amounts that you have determined to assign to each trust. This will greatly help you in your decision-making as you get near the end.

Here are some quirks to keep in mind while doing this split:

1. There may be accrued interest associated with savings accounts, bonds, and certificates of deposit. It may not have been added to your account by the bank or your brokerage firm, but it is part of your assets. Be sure to include this interest in your calculations. The Internal Revenue Service will want it included if you file an estate tax return.

2. If any of your stocks were ex-dividend on the date of death, be sure to include these dividends as part of the assets. Ex-dividend means that dividends have been declared by a company, but have not yet been paid to the shareholders. These unpaid dividends are an asset of the trust.

3. In order to obtain the correct totals for each trust, you will probably have to split one or more of the assets between the trusts. Your spreadsheet will help you to do this.

Retitling the Assets With Splitting of Trust

The letters necessary to transfer the assets to the proper trusts are essentially the same letters that were used earlier in this chapter to illustrate how to retitle assets where there is no trust split. Instead of repeating them, I'll explain the minor changes.

When you designate the trust's name for registering the new title, include the name of the separate trust that the asset has been assigned to. Be sure to use the same name as designated in the trust document. If you are unsure, ask your attorney for the proper designation. For example, if the asset were to go into Trust A you would direct it to be re-registered as:

(Your name), trustee
(Name of trust) dated (date of original trust), Trust A

Be sure to provide the proper social security number or taxpayer ID number (if Trust B).

Everything else will be the same.

For the assets, which will be split between the trusts, the letters need to be modified to provide exact directions for the split.

Managing Your Trusts After the Split

Once you have completed the transfers and retitling of your assets to the different trusts, you probably feel that your job is completed and that you deserve a rest. It is probably true that you deserve a rest, but don't put aside the trusts and feel that your work is over.

In order to maintain the identification of your Trust B as a separate entity, you must treat it as a separate entity. Chapter 6 will guide you through the operations and Chapter 7 will give you the tax guidance.

Don't fall into the trap of thinking that just because the surviving spouse may receive all the benefits of both trusts and may even control both trusts as the trustee, they can be operated together. Keep excellent records of the assets in Trust B. Treat it like a business. Maintain a separate checking account to transfer income to the surviving spouse.

It may seem to be a little cumbersome, but it can convince the Internal Revenue Service and possibly disgruntled heirs that Trust B truly is separate and must be legally recognized as separate. This ensures both your estate tax benefits and avoidance of probate. The trustmaker paid fees to set up this trust in order to get the benefits. Don't lose what was paid for.

CHAPTER 11

■ ■ ■ ■ ■ ■ ■ ■ ■

Managing the Revocable Living Trust Upon the Death of the Trustmaker(s)

The job of the successor trustee usually begins after the death of the trustmaker or, in the case of revocable living trust set up by a married couple, the death of the surviving spouse. This is often a very emotional time for the successor trustee since the trustmaker was probably a relative or close friend.

The first thing to remember as you take over the management of the trust's assets is that in most cases, you don't have to rush. Take your time; let the emotions subside and take a logical, step-by-step approach to the task ahead.

Understand the Trust

Your first step is to become familiar with the trust, its assets, and your duties. READ THE TRUST. Review Chapters 2 and 4 of this book to learn what is expected of a trustee.

If possible, review the trust with the trustmaker's advisors. The attorney, financial, and tax advisors should be able to give you directions as to the intent of the trustmakers as well as a list of assets that are in the trust. Do this, even if you plan to use your own advisors while administering the trust. You will find their insight valuable.

Trustee/Executor

As you study the trust and other documents, you will find that there is another player in the game, the executor for the estate of the deceased. Very often, you will have the dual role of both executor and trustee, but you may also find that the trustmaker named someone else in the will as the executor. While the two roles are similar, there are different responsibilities for each in the final settlement and closing of the estate. If the executor is different than the successor trustee, the two will need to cooperate to make this transitional period smooth and easy.

As we go through the process, I'll indicate which action is the responsibility of the executor and which is the responsibility of the trustee.

Gathering the Assets

Once you understand the trust and your responsibilities as successor trustee, it is time to determine the assets that belong to the trust. Hopefully the trustmaker did a good job and maintained an accurate record of the trust's assets. Don't count on it. You will probably turn up some surprises as you work through this stage.

As you gather the information to develop your inventory, you will find that the assets fall in several categories of ownership.

1. *Assets owned by the trust and properly titled in the name of the trust.* These are the easiest assets to work with since they are already in the trust. By the terms of the trust, you have legal control of the assets. All that is necessary is to notify the proper re-registering authority.

In the case where you are taking over a trust that had the A- and B-type components that were discussed in Chapter 10, you will have subcategories: Trust A assets and Trust B assets. Make sure you keep these assets separated as you take over control of the trust.

2. *Assets owned by the trust but not registered in the name of the trust.* These items are generally personal property such as clothing, jewelry, furniture, and collectibles that do not have a registered title. Read the trust. There probably is a general transfer clause that placed these assets in the trust.

3. *Assets owned by the trustmaker, not by the trust.* Often a trustmaker will make an investment and not register it in the trust's name. Sometimes an asset may have been overlooked when the original transfers to the trust were made. Maybe the omission was intentional and the trustmaker decided not to place something in the trust. Whatever the reason, these assets are controlled by the executor under the terms of the will.

Most wills prepared in conjunction with a revocable living trust state very simply that any assets not in the trust will be "poured over" to the trust upon the death of the trustmaker. That is why they are usually called *pour-over wills.* Don't take them for granted. There may also be other provisions in the will that the executor must follow. Titled assets not already in the trust may need to be transferred to the trust though a probate process.

4. *Assets controlled by contracts.* These are the assets that are passed on to heirs by terms of written contracts. They may be owned by the trust or they may have been owned by the trust-maker as an individual. Examples of these assets are:

a. Pensions/profit-sharing plans

b. Annuities

c. Individual retirement accounts (IRA's)

d. Deferred compensation plans
  - 401(k)'s
  - 403(b)'s
  - Savings plans sponsored by employers

e. Life insurance policies

As trustee, you are interested in these contracts, as the trust may be named as beneficiary. An executor is interested because the estate may be the beneficiary, either by name or by default if no beneficiary is named. In addition, these assets must be included in any estate or state death tax returns that are required.

Where to Look for the Assets

In addition to the filing cabinet, trust notebook, or properly prepared list, there are several other resources you can use to make sure that you have located all of the assets.

1. *Income tax returns.* You will find many clues here. This would include both the personal income tax return (Form 1040) and the fiduciary tax return (Form 1041) for Trust B if you are working with a previously split trust. All interest and dividend income should be listed, including the name of who paid the income. The return will also provide you with the names of all partnerships that are involved.

If you see the name of a stock brokerage listed, this is a good indication that there may be a stock account.

Look for an indication of pension or IRA income. If there is, there should be a Form 1099-R with the return indicating the source of this income.

2. *Check registers and cancelled checks.* Look for any indications of deposits from investments or payments made to purchase or support investments. Payments made to an out-of-the-area tax collector may indicate real estate that is owned. This will also give you an idea of where non-interest-bearing checking accounts may have been held.

3. *Estate tax return (Form 706).* If the trustmaker had been married and was the surviving spouse, there may have been an estate tax return filed upon the death of the first spouse. This would list all of the assets that the first spouse had an ownership

interest at the time of death. Although many assets could have been sold or given away since then, you may find some clues.

4. *Other family members.* Check with other family members for possible clues.

5. *The trustmaker's advisors.* Make sure that you verify with the following that you know about all of the assets they have a record of:

   a. Attorney

   b. Financial planner

   c. Accountant/tax preparer

   d. Stockbroker

   e. Insurance agent

Managing the Trust Assets

Now that you have found all the assets it is time to again READ THE TRUST. You need to determine what you should do with them. Are you going to be a short-term caretaker, holding the assets just long enough to properly distribute them to heirs? Or will you be operating the trust for an extended period of time to fulfill the instructions of the trustmaker?

In either case, you have the fiduciary responsibility to properly manage all of the assets. You could be held responsible by any of the heirs for losses due to imprudent management. Again, review Chapters 2 and 4 of this book.

Income Tax Responsibilities

You may find the income tax situation appears to be a little complicated, particularly in the year that the trustmaker died. Don't let it overwhelm you. If you take the time to look at it logically, the requirements do make sense.

In the typical revocable living trust situation, you could be filing up to four separate sets of income tax returns. They will not be any more difficult than usual if you have maintained the proper records.

Keep in mind the various tax reporting entities that you are dealing with, as well as the time periods that they owned assets and earned income. Then you will see the logic in the various returns.

Let's start with the easiest to understand. *A final tax return, Form 1040, must be filed for the deceased trustmaker* if sufficient income was earned to require filing (if total income including sales price of capital assets exceeds the sum of the allowable standard deduction and personal exemption for the year), if taxes had been withheld from any income during the year, or if estimated tax payments had been made. I prefer to file a return, even if one is not required, to inform the Internal Revenue Service that they should close the books on this account and not to expect further returns. This return is the responsibility of the executor, if appointed, and should be signed by the executor. If you are both trustee and executor, be sure to sign as executor and not as trustee.

All income and deductions for the deceased trustmaker stop as of the date of death. You will prorate all interest earned. It must be calculated as of the date of death. Interest earned on accounts after the date of death is reported by the trust or the estate, as explained later. Dividends are calculated as of the ex-dividend date, which is the date that stock must be owned in order to collect dividends. Dividends with an ex-dividend date before the date of

Frank and Ernest

176

death belong to the trustmaker. Salaries and business income earned prior to death also belong to the trustmaker.

It is a little more difficult to determine the exact proration of partnership income, particularly from investment partnerships. From a practical standpoint, the best way is to prorate the income reported on the K-1 statements based on the date of death unless you have sufficient information for a different split.

There is one tax break provided for deceased taxpayers. A full year's personal exemption and standard deduction (if used) are available, without proration, no matter when the death occurred.

If the final return has a refund, be sure to attach Form 1310, "Statement of Person Claiming Refund Due a Deceased Taxpayer." A copy of this form is included in the appendix (page 247). Without this form, you will not be able to collect any refund due to the estate.

In order to make sure that the Internal Revenue Service will properly handle this tax return, write "DECEASED" and the date of death on the top of the front page of Form 1040.

If the trustmaker died prior to filing the previous year's tax return, the executor is also responsible for filing that tax return. Indicate "DECEASED" and the date of death on the top of this return also.

The remaining income tax returns are all filed on Form 1041 (fiduciary tax return). The first of these is the *return for the estate* and is the responsibility of the executor. This return reports all income earned by any assets that were not in the trust as of the date of death. If all assets were in the trust at that time, this return will not be necessary. Income and deductions will be prorated as of the date of death and will cease when each asset is either transferred to the trust or distributed to the beneficiaries. The major difference between filing a Form 1041 for an estate and for a trust is that you may choose a more convenient tax year-end for an estate. A trust must use December 31 as the year-end but an estate may choose any month-end to close out its tax year as long as the first year is no longer than twelve months.

The next return to be filed on Form 1041 will be the *Trust B return,* if there was a previous split. This will be the same type of return that has been filed previously for this trust, if Trust B had been implemented upon the death of the first spouse. All income that had been distributed to the trustmaker before death will be reported on the Schedule K-1 for the trustmaker. All distributions to beneficiaries will be reported on their own K-1's.

The last of this group of returns is the Form 1041 *return for the trust.* This may be Trust A if there had been a previous split, or it may be the entire trust if no split had occurred in the past. The return will report all income and deductions earned by the trust, starting with the day after the death of the trustmaker. You will also add in any income from assets transferred in from the estate, such as stocks and bank accounts, as of the date of transfer.

Other Tasks

There are some other administrative matters that you must take care of. You will need taxpayer ID numbers for the newly irrevocable trust and the estate (if there is one) before you can notify the investments of the change in status or file the income tax returns. If the trust had been split by a previous death, there will be no need to obtain a new taxpayer ID number for Trust B. The trustmaker's social security number is no longer valid. Use Internal Revenue Service Form SS-4 to obtain these numbers. A copy of this form is in the appendix (page 236).

You also need to notify the Internal Revenue Service that you now have the fiduciary responsibility for the trust(s) and the estate, if applicable. Form 56 is used to report this information. It can also be found in the appendix (page 237).

There may be some confusion when comparing the interest and dividends earned by the various entities and the amounts reported by the financial institution on the Form 1099's. The 1099's for the deceased trustmaker's social security number will include all earnings up to the point that the financial institution transferred the assets to either the trust or the beneficiaries. This should not be of any concern to you. Because you marked "DECEASED" on the top of the Form 1040, the Internal Revenue Service will know that they will be unable to match 1099's to what is reported on the Form 1040.

One way to avoid potential inquiries from the Internal Revenue Service is to report the full amounts as reported on Form 1099 on the decedent's return and then subtract the trust and/or estate portion as "Nominee Interest" or "Nominee Dividends." This will give the correct net amount. Here is an example for interest reported on Schedule B of Form 1040.

First National Bank	$ 200
Second State Bank	+ 400
Less (nominee interest, Trust 12-3456789)	– (450)

At the bottom of the section, on Schedule B, you would indicate the corrected net amount of $150.

Form 706—Estate Tax Return

The estate tax is not an income tax, but a tax on the privilege of transferring your assets to your heirs. It requires an inventory of all assets and an accurate listing of their values as of the date of death. As an alternative, you can use the value six months after death. The date you choose must be the same for all assets.

This 44-page form must be filed within nine months of the date of death (unless you request an extension) together with payment of any estate tax that is due. The executor is responsible for this task. If you are both the successor trustee and executor, it will be your responsibility to file this report.

This is one of the more complex tax forms to prepare. Seek the assistance of an attorney or qualified tax preparer who has had experience with filing Form 706. Due to the potentially high amount of taxes that may be due, each Form 706 is manually reviewed by senior Internal Revenue Service agents and a large percentage are audited.

The Tax Reform Act of 1997 raised the minimum level of assets required before filing a Form 706. Prior to 1998, the level was $600,000. This is scheduled to be increased in steps to $1,000,000 by 2006. Check with your advisors as to the threshold that applies to your situation. Chapter 8, page 86, has a schedule of these amounts.

Valuation of Assets

One of the critical tasks for the successor trustee and/or executor is to obtain the correct values for all assets that belonged to the deceased trustmaker. These values will be used for many different purposes in the future.

You will need the correct values to file Form 706, if that is required. The correct values are also needed to establish the tax cost basis if any of these assets are sold by the estate, trust, or the heirs at any time in the future. A third purpose is to provide the cost information for any charitable gifting of these assets.

The easiest way to value *listed stocks and mutual funds* is to save the *Wall Street Journal* (or any newspaper that carries all of the stocks and funds involved) with the opening and closing prices for the date of death. If the trustmaker died on a day that the stock market was closed, you will need to average the prices for the business day before death and the business day after death.

If you are unable to find the correct prices, call the stockbroker or financial planner who handled these accounts. They should be able to obtain this information for you. For mutual funds, call the Shareholder Services telephone number listed on your statement for these values.

Bonds and unlisted stocks require a little more effort to get the correct value. Your easiest source is your stockbroker or financial planner. The sooner you contact them after the death, the easier it will be to obtain these values.

As a last resort, contact an evaluation service such as Evaluation Services Inc. to obtain stock, bond, and mutual fund values. They are located at 180 Old Tappan Road, Old Tappan, NJ 07675. Their phone number is 201-784-8500.

For *annuities,* it is a simple procedure to call the insurance company and ask for the valuation as of the date of death. The telephone number is usually on your statement. You can also ask your financial planner, stockbroker, or insurance agent to get this value for you.

Real estate is a little more difficult. There is no telephone number to call for a value. You should get an appraisal from a qualified appraiser. This will cost you a fee, but it is worth it. Many times you may feel that your real estate agent can give you a good estimate. This estimate may be accurate, but if there is a question in a subsequent audit, the Internal Revenue Service will also obtain an appraisal. Their appraisal will stand up in a dispute better than a real estate agent's estimate.

For *jewelry, collectibles, antiques, and other special items,* it is best to get an appraisal.

You may be able to avail yourself of a court-appointed probate appraiser. Their fees are generally lower than independent appraisers. Check with your attorney to see if this is possible.

Charitable Gifts

A normal instinct for a successor trustee is to give away many of the personal items of the deceased trustmaker. These items often include clothing, furniture, and other tangible items. Be very careful when doing this. READ THE TRUST and also read the will. The trust and/or estate can only make charitable contributions if specifically authorized to do so in the trust or will. Just like bank accounts and investments, these personal items are part of the trust and your responsibility.

If the trust or will does not allow you to donate these items to charity, coordinate with the beneficiaries and determine their desires. The easiest way to dispose of any unwanted assets is to report to the beneficiaries that you have distributed these items by making a donation to charity in their name. Send the receipts to the beneficiaries, together with a listing of the items and their values. The beneficiaries can now take a charitable deduction on their personal tax returns. Before doing this, obtain approval from all of the beneficiaries.

Managing the Assets

If the trust requires that the assets or a portion of them remain in the trust for an extended period of time, you must manage them for the benefit of the beneficiaries. Review Chapters 2 and 4 for guidance in this area.

Transferring Non-Trust Assets to the Trust

If there are any assets that the trustmaker did not previously transfer to the trust, but are bequeathed by the will to the trust, you must make sure that they are transferred in an orderly manner. It is the responsibility of the executor of the estate to follow the proper probate procedures to complete this transfer. At the same time, it is the responsibility of the trustee to make sure that the trust receives all that it deserves.

Make use of your attorney in this area to ensure that this is handled correctly.

Retitling Trust Assets

Even though the trust assets are already in the trust, the various transfer agents should be notified that you are now the trustee. This will simplify future transfers and other transactions, as well as change the address on the investments if you desire mailings to your own home or office. They also need to know the correct taxpayer ID number.

The first step is to obtain a taxpayer ID number for the trust (Trust A if it had previously been split). This is essential for proper Internal Revenue Service reporting. Use Form ss-4 to do this.

Once you have obtained your taxpayer ID number, you will follow a format similar to the initial transfer of the assets to the trust and the split into the A/B Trusts if that had occurred.

Although this notification should be accomplished as soon as possible, here is a time-saving option that you should consider. If the trust calls for an immediate transfer of assets to the beneficiaries, you may be able to combine the notification and transfer steps into one step. You should consider this only if the transfers are to take place within a relatively short time frame after the death and not carry forward to the next tax year. Sample letters and checklists for this are included in Chapter 12.

Use checklists 11-1 and 11-2 as your guide for the overall process of retitling.

■ Real Estate

There is no real need to retitle real estate until a sale or transfer is ready to take place. At that time, it will be important for whoever is conducting the title search (generally an attorney or title company) that you are able to provide a clear chain of title.

Checklist 11-1
RETITLING ASSETS FOR SUCCESSOR TRUSTEE
AFTER DEATH OF TRUSTMAKER

Action	Completed
1. Read the trust	
2. Prepare/review list of assets to be retitled	
3. Obtain new taxpayer ID number (Form ss-4)	
4. Verify that Form 56 is filed	
5. Retitle assets (see individual checklists)	
6. Notify: a. Accountant/tax preparer	
b. Financial advisor	
c. Attorney	
d. Beneficiaries	

Checklist 11-2
SAMPLE LISTING OF ASSETS TO BE RETITLED
AFTER DEATH OF TRUSTMAKER

Asset	Paperwork submitted	Retitle complete
Vacant land—Lake Smith		
Home—123 Main Street		
XYZ mutual fund		
ABC stock		
Stock brokerage account		
CD at local bank		

This would include a copy of the trust, any death certificates, and all paperwork showing the validity of your position as trustee. This would include any amendments to the trust and resignation or appointments of trustees.

There are three organizations that you should inform of your status as trustee and your address. The first is the local county tax collector. You are responsible for maintaining the property tax payments. As a fiduciary, you could be held personally liable for any penalties and interest resulting from late payments.

The other two organizations that need to be notified are the mortgage holder(s), if any, and the homeowner's insurance company. You also need to keep these payments current.

Sample letters 11-1, 11-2, and 11-3 will guide you in these notifications.

Letter 11-1 will notify the tax collector of the new address and taxpayer ID number of the trust. Now you can receive future billings in a timely manner. It also requests verification on the status of past payments to prevent any surprises later.

Since you are not changing the title at this point, no notary acknowledgment or signature guarantee should be required.

If more than one piece of property is located within the same county, I recommend that you send a separate letter for each parcel. This can prevent confusion and possible oversight of one or more of the parcels by the tax collector's office.

The easiest way to notify your homeowner's insurance carrier is to call the agent (or the insurance company if the policy is written by a company that does not use agents). Each insurance company has its own procedures and forms. It may be necessary to make some changes in the policy, particularly if a property is changing from owner-occupied to a rental or unoccupied building. If you prefer to do this change by letter, follow sample letter 11-3.

Sample Letter 11-1
NOTIFICATION OF COUNTY TAX COLLECTOR
UPON DEATH OF TRUSTMAKER

Name of the trust
Your address
City, state, zip code

Date letter written

Tax collector
Name of county
Their address
Their city, state, zip code

Ref: (How the property is referenced on the tax bill)

Dear Sir/Madam:

I am the successor trustee of the (name of trust) dated (date of the trust). The previous trustee, (name of trustmaker), died on (date of death).

Please send all future tax billings and notices to:

(Your name), trustee
(Name of trust) dated (date of trust)
Trustee's address
Trustee's city, state, zip code

The taxpayer identification number for the trust is now 12-3456789.

Please inform me of the current status of this account and the date and amount of the next payment that is due.

This change does not constitute a change of ownership of this property and no new assessment is required.

Please acknowledge these changes.

Sincerely,

_____

(Your name), trustee

Sample Letter 11-2
NOTIFICATION OF MORTGAGE LENDER
UPON DEATH OF TRUSTMAKER

Name of trust
Your address
City, state, zip code

Date letter written

Name of mortgage lender
Their address
Their city, state, zip code

Ref: (Account number)

Dear Sir/Madam:

I am the successor trustee of the (name of the trust) dated (date of the trust). This trust is the owner of the property secured by the above-referenced loan. The previous trustee, (name of trustmaker), died on (date of death).

Please send all future billings and notices to:

(Your name), trustee
(Name of trust) dated (date of trust)
Trustee's address
Trustee's city, state, zip code

The taxpayer identification number for the trust is now 12-3456789.

Please inform me of the current status of this loan and the date and amount of the next payment that is due.

Please acknowledge these changes.

Sincerely,

_____

(Your name), trustee

Sample Letter 11-3
NOTIFICATION OF PROPERTY INSURANCE COMPANY
UPON DEATH OF TRUSTMAKER

Name of trust
Your address
City, state, zip code

Date letter written

Name of insurance company
Their address
Their city, state, zip code

Ref: Policy (number)

Dear Sir/Madam:

I am the successor trustee of the (name of the trust) dated (date of the trust). This trust is the owner of the property insured by the above-referenced policy. The previous trustee, (name of trustmaker), died on (date of death).

Please send all future billings and notices to:

(Your name), trustee
(Name of trust) dated (date of trust)
Trustee's address
Trustee's city, state, zip code

The taxpayer identification number for the trust is now 12-3456789.

Please inform me of the current status of this policy and the date and amount of the next payment due.

Please acknowledge these changes.

Sincerely,

_____

(Your name), trustee

Checklist 11-3
RETITLING OF REAL ESTATE AFTER DEATH OF TRUSTMAKER
Property _____

Action	Completed
1. Read the trust	
2. Locate the deed	
3. Locate current tax bill	
4. Locate mortgage payment records	
5. Locate insurance policy	
6. Notify tax collector and receive acknowledgment	
7. Notify mortgage holder and receive acknowledgment	
8. Notify insurance agent/company and receive acknowledgment	

■ Mutual Funds, Brokerage Accounts, Managed Accounts, and Limited Partnerships

You can use letters that are very similar to the transfer letters found in Chapter 10 to complete this task. Most limited partnerships will require their own forms to complete the retitling, and some may also want you to sign their special forms. Many limited partnerships will charge a fee in the range of $25 to $50 to do any change in a title, but some will waive the fee if the change is due to a death.

Sample letter 11-4 provides the securities firm with the documentation it should need to complete retitling. It gives the reason for the change and verification by means of the death certificate.

Sample Letter 11-4
RETITLING OF ASSETS AFTER DEATH OF TRUSTMAKER —
MUTUAL FUNDS, MANAGED ACCOUNTS, BROKERAGE
ACCOUNTS, LIMITED PARTNERSHIPS

Name of trust
Your address
City, state, zip code

Date letter written

(Mutual fund company, stock brokerage, etc.)
Their address
Their city, state, zip code

Ref: (Name of investment) (account number) — (could be more
than one if same mutual fund/limited partnership company)

Dear Sir/Madam:

I am the successor trustee of the (name of the trust) dated (date of
the trust). The previous trustee, (name of previous trustee), died on
(date of death). I request that the above-referenced account(s) be
re-registered as follows:

(Your name), trustee
(Name of trust) dated (date trust was signed)
Trustee's address
Trustee's city, state, zip code

The taxpayer identification number for the trust (will remain the
same [or] has been changed to 12-3456789).

Enclosed is the following:

1. Form W-9
2. Certified copy of the death certificate of (name of deceased trustee)
3. Notarized affidavit of domicile
4. (Appropriate pages of trust designating you as successor trustee).

(For limited partnerships add this paragraph:)

I understand that since this is not a transfer of ownership and the
retitling is due to the death of the owner, there are no transfer fees
for this change.

Sincerely,

_____
(Your name), trustee

* Have signature Medallion-guaranteed.

Be sure to send an original certified copy of the death certificate with the official seal. Photocopies are not acceptable to most transfer agencies.

The notarized affidavit of domicile verifies which state laws govern the transfer. (A copy is shown on page 137.)

Even though in some cases the taxpayer ID number remains the same (such as changing the trustee in Trust B), it is easier to verify this number with a new W-9 signed by the current trustee. If the transfer agent doesn't have satisfactory verification of this number they are required to withhold 31% federal tax withholding on all income and sale proceeds.

The signature guarantee on this letter is used to protect the transfer agent from the liability of a fraudulent transfer. The firm providing this Medallion guarantee has a bond to repay the transfer agent for any losses. You can obtain this signature guarantee from a firm participating in the Medallion program such as a

Checklist 11-4
RETITLING MUTUAL FUNDS, BROKERAGE ACCOUNTS, MANAGED ACCOUNTS AND LIMITED PARTNERSHIPS AFTER THE DEATH OF THE TRUSTMAKER

Name of Asset _____

Action	Completed
1. Read the trust	
2. Write letter (11-4)	
3. Successor trustee sign (signature guaranteed)	
4. Mail letter	
5. Complete additional requirements	
6. Receive acknowledgment of completed transfer	

stock brokerage, member of the National Association of Securities Dealers, and some banks.

■ Individual Stock/Bond Certificates

The procedure for retitling individual stock certificates follows closely the steps taken to retitle the previous assets. The major difference is that you must surrender your current certificate so that a new one can be issued. If you can't find the certificate, follow the instructions in the next section.

One extra step you will have to take with this retitling is determining the transfer agent responsible for maintaining the records for each of these certificates. Most companies do not maintain the records of the stockholders or bondholders. Instead, they use an outside transfer agent to perform this service. You can usually find the name and address of this transfer agent from your latest dividend check or the annual report. If you cannot find one of these, ask your stockbroker or financial planner for assistance. Another avenue for you to use is to call the company directly and ask for the information from their shareholder services department.

In order to retitle any certificate, the transfer agent requires your signature on either the back of the certificate or on a separate form called a *stock/bond power*. Both say essentially the same thing, that you are transferring title. Some advisors recommend that you use the separate stock power to make it more difficult for an illegal transfer if the material gets lost in the mail. Your signature on the stock/bond power or the back of the stock certificate must be guaranteed through the Medallion program, just like your letter.

You should mail the letter with your certificate(s) by registered, insured U.S. Mail since these are negotiable documents. Insure the letter for 2% of the value. If it is lost in the mail, you will be able to get new certificates if you post a bond at a cost of about 2% of the value.

Sample Letter 11-5
RETITLING INDIVIDUAL STOCK AND BOND CERTIFICATES
AFTER DEATH OF TRUSTMAKER

(Name of trust) dated (date trust was signed)
Your address
City, state, zip code

Date letter written

Transfer agent
Their address
Their city, state, zip code

Ref: (Name of corporation), (CUSIP number), (number of shares), (certificate number(s))

Dear Sir/Madam:

I am the successor trustee of the (name of the trust) dated (date of the trust). The previous trustee, (name of previous trustee), died on (date of death). I request that the above-referenced and enclosed certificate(s) be re-registered and reissued as follows:

(Your name), trustee
(Name of trust) dated (date of the original trust)
Trustee's address
Trustee's city, state, zip code

The taxpayer ID number for the trust (will remain the same [or] has been changed to 12-3456789).

In addition to the certificate(s), enclosed are the following:

1. Stock/bond power(s) (if used)
2. Form W-9
3. Certified copy of the death certificate of (name of deceased trustee)
4. Notarized affidavit of domicile
5. (Appropriate pages of trust designating you as successor trustee).

Sincerely,

_____

(Your name), trustee

* Have signature Medallion-guaranteed.

The CUSIP number identifies the stock or bond, the company that issued it, and the particular class or series of the security.

The reason for photocopying the certificate is to give you a backup record of the certificate with the CUSIP number in case the certificate is lost or stolen in the future.

There is an easier way to handle these transfers. Have your financial planner or stockbroker open an account in the name of the trust. Deposit the certificates. Then have the account re-registered in the same manner discussed earlier with checklist 11-4 and sample letter 11-4. This way you can transfer all certificates at once and not worry about loss or theft in the mail.

Checklist 11-5
RETITLING STOCK/BOND CERTIFICATES UPON
THE DEATH OF TRUSTMAKER
Name of Stock/Bond _____

Action	Completed
1. Read the trust	
2. Locate certificate/bond	
3. Determine transfer agent and address	
4. Write letter (11-5)	
5. Sign (signature guaranteed)	
6. Sign stock certificate/bond/stock power (signature guaranteed)	
7. Mail letters by registered insured U.S. Mail	
8. Receive new certificate	
9. Photocopy certificate	
10. Safely store certificate	

■ Lost Stock/Bond Certificates

One of the main reasons I like using a stock brokerage account for maintaining stock and bond certificates is that you can't misplace the certificates. If you do determine that the previous trustee/trustmaker misplaced some certificates, all is not lost. You can replace them. It just takes a little more effort.

The transfer agent will have a record of the shares. You must notify them of the ownership, the loss, and the retitling of the certificates. This may require a few months to complete. The more information you can provide, the easier the retitling will be.

Checklist 11-11
RETITLING LOST STOCK/BOND CERTIFICATES
UPON DEATH OF TRUSTMAKER
Name of Stock/Bond _____

Action	Completed
1. Read the trust	
2. Determine number of shares owned	
3. Determine transfer agent and address	
4. Write letter (11-6)	
5. Sign (signature guaranteed)	
6. Mail letter	
7. Receive instructions/forms from transfer agent	
8. Return required forms with check for bond to transfer agent	
9. Receive new certificates	
10. Photocopy certificates	
11. Safely store certificates	

Sample Letter 11-6
RETITLING LOST STOCK/BOND CERTIFICATES
UPON THE DEATH OF THE TRUSTMAKER

(Name of trust)
Your address
City, state, zip code

Date letter written

Transfer agent
Their address
Their city, state, zip code
Ref: (Name of corporation), (CUSIP number if known), (number of shares if known), (certificate number(s) if known)

Dear Sir/Madam:

I am the successor trustee of the (name of the trust) dated (date of the trust). The previous trustee, (name of previous trustee), died on (date of death). The trust is the owner of (number of shares if known) shares in the above-referenced company. I am unable to locate the certificate(s).

I request that these shares be reissued and re-registered as follows:

(Your name), trustee
(Name of trust) dated (date of the original trust)
Trustee's address
Trustee's city, state, zip code

The taxpayer identification number for the trust (will remain the same [or] has been changed to 12-3456789).

Enclosed are the following:

1. Form W-9
2. Certified copy of the death certificate of (name of deceased trustee)
3. Notarized affidavit of domicile
4. (Appropriate pages of trust designating you as successor trustee).

Please forward any additional requirements to my address above.

Sincerely,

_____

(Your name), trustee

* Have signature Medallion-guaranteed.

Use sample letter 11-6 to guide you. The transfer agent will normally require you to fill in their forms and provide a bond to protect them in case the certificates show up at a later date. The cost of the bond is usually about 2% of the value. The transfer agent will notify you of the exact cost of the bond.

■ Annuities

When you have annuities involved with the trust and the estate, you must be careful and learn what role the trust is playing. The trust could be the owner of the annuity, the beneficiary of the annuity, both owner and beneficiary, or neither owner nor beneficiary. It all depends on how the annuity was set up.

You've been told many times to READ THE TRUST. Now I'm going to tell you to READ THE ANNUITY. This is because not all annuity contracts are the same. You must determine the owner of the contract, the annuitant, and the beneficiaries. You can usually find these listed either on a page called "specification page" or on a copy of the original application attached to the contract.

Most annuities are designed to provide an income for a set period of time, or for the lifetime of an individual (the annuitant). This must be a natural person (or persons), and the trust cannot be the annuitant. Normally the death of the annuitant or the owner will trigger the distribution of the value of the contract to the beneficiaries. Some policies will name a co-annuitant or a contingent annuitant to allow the contract to remain in place without triggering a distribution to beneficiaries upon the death of the annuitant.

If the trustmaker was listed as the annuitant, it is likely that the contract value will be distributed after the trustmaker's death.

The trustmaker could have been the owner of the annuity with another individual named as the annuitant. If this is the case, you need to read the annuity to find out what action is triggered by the trustmaker's death. The annuity contract may be designed to stay in force with a new owner (the trust or someone else) named or, upon death, the annuity value may be transferred to the beneficiaries.

If the trust is the owner of the annuity, the trustee has the primary responsibility for taking action. If the trustmaker was the owner, the executor is responsible. In either case, if there are named beneficiaries, there is no need for probate; the terms of the annuity contract are the controlling factors.

As trustee and/or executor you should contact the insurance company that issued the contract, notify them of the death of the trustmaker, and arrange for the proper disposition of the annuity. If the value is to be distributed to beneficiaries (either the trust or named individuals), make arrangements for this distribution.

Life insurance companies always have their own death benefit claim forms. I have found that the easiest way to proceed with annuities is to call the life insurance company directly and request the proper claim forms. If you need help with this, contact the investment advisor or insurance agent who originally placed the trustmaker in the annuity.

There are tax consequences which you should consider when requesting the proceeds from an annuity. All gain is subject to income tax in the year received. The gain on an annuity contract is the difference between the cost of the annuity and the amount received. Even though these gains are normally subject to a 10% early withdrawal penalty tax if withdrawn before age 59½, this penalty tax is waived when received as a death benefit.

If the trust calls for immediate distribution of assets to the beneficiaries, you want to delay receipt of the annuity proceeds until the year that you actually make distributions. This way you will ensure that the proceeds are taxed at the beneficiary's rates rather than the higher trust income tax rates.

Checklist 11-7
ANNUITIES AFTER DEATH OF TRUSTMAKER
Annuity Contract _____

Action	Completed
1. Read the trust	
2. Read the annuity	
3. Determine function of trustmaker	
4. Determine function of trust	
5. Contact advisor/insurance company	
6. Receive forms from insurance company	
7. Return completed forms to insurance company and forward to beneficiaries	
8. Receive proceeds from annuity contract if trust is the beneficiary	

■ Life Insurance Policies

As trustee, you are responsible for collecting the proceeds of all life insurance policies that name the trust as the beneficiary. You will also probably take the lead in ensuring the distribution of proceeds to other named beneficiaries.

There are no *income tax* consequences involved with life insurance benefits except for any interest earned from the date of death until the date actually paid by the life insurance company.

There may be severe *estate tax* consequences that you need to be aware of if you are also the executor of the estate. The proceeds of any policy that is considered to have been owned by the decedent will be included in his or her estate and subject to estate tax. This would include policies owned directly by the trustmaker and also policies owned by a revocable trust. If you have any questions on your particular situation, review it with your advisors.

Your first step is to gather up all the life insurance policies. Read the policies to determine both the ownership and the beneficiaries. Inform the beneficiaries that they will be receiving forms to make their claims.

Contact the life insurance agent for each policy to start the claims process. If there is no agent available, contact the life insurance company directly. Request the necessary death benefit claim forms. As trustee, you are responsible for filing all claims for policies that name the trust as the beneficiary.

Checklist 11-8
LIFE INSURANCE CLAIMS AFTER DEATH OF TRUSTMAKER
Life Policy _____

Action	Completed
1. Read the trust	
2. Read the policy	
3. Determine ownership	
4. Determine beneficiaries	
5. Contact insurance agent or life insurance company	
6. Obtain claim forms	
7. Distribute claim forms to beneficiaries	
8. Fill in claim form for trust as beneficiary	
9. Collect policy benefits	
10. Deposit policy benefits	

Look for any life insurance policies that the trust or the trust-maker may have owned that insured the life of another person. You will not be able to collect a death benefit if the insured is still alive. The policy itself will be an asset of the trust and may need to be included in the inventory of assets on the estate tax return.

If you do find a policy on the life of someone else, contact the insurance agent or life insurance company and obtain the necessary form to transfer ownership to you as trustee of the trust. You may also have to change the beneficiary of the policy.

■ IRA's, Pensions, and Other Qualified Retirement Plans

These assets would have been owned directly by the trustmaker and would not have been assets of the trust. The trust may be the named beneficiary for one or more of these accounts.

This is an area where it is often a little more difficult to obtain complete records. If you do not have a good listing from the trust-maker, check with his or her former employer to see if there are any residual pension benefits and who is the beneficiary. Look for a Form 1099-R attached to any tax return for records of withdrawals. Check with the trustmaker's advisors for a listing of known accounts.

Since these pension-type assets do not belong to the trust, it is the responsibility of the executor to handle them. However, the trustee is still responsible for claiming all benefits due to the trust. If you are not both the trustee and the executor, cooperation between the two is vital here.

Depending on the amount of information available, it may be easier to make the initial contact by telephone or by letter. The sample letters that follow will guide you through this process.

These letters should set the wheels in motion for the disbursement of any death benefits. There is no need for a Form W-9, death certificate, or affidavit of domicile since the responsible company will send you their requirements. Signature guarantees are not necessary either.

Sample Letter 11-7
CONTACT WITH QUALIFIED PENSION PLAN IF
BENEFITS AND/OR BENEFICIARIES ARE UNKNOWN
UPON DEATH OF TRUSTMAKER

Your name, executor
Estate of (name of trustmaker)
Your address
City, state, zip code

Date letter written

Name of IRA or plan administrator
Their address
Their city, state, zip code

Ref: (Name of plan, IRA, etc.), FBO (name of trustmaker), (account number if known)

Dear Sir/Madam:

I am the executor of the estate of (name of the trustmaker), who died on (date of death). (Name of trustmaker) was the owner of the above-referenced retirement account.

Please forward to my address above information concerning the following:

1. Any death benefits payable to the estate or other beneficiaries
2. The names of any beneficiaries
3. Options for receipt of death benefits
4. Necessary forms for application for receipt of these benefits.

Sincerely,

_____

(Your name), executor

(FBO means "for the benefit of.")

Sample Letter 11-8
CONTACT WITH QUALIFIED PENSION PLAN
IF BENEFICIARIES ARE KNOWN
UPON DEATH OF TRUSTMAKER

Your name, executor
Estate of (name of trustmaker)
Your address
City, state, zip code

Date letter written

Name of IRA or plan administrator
Their address
Their city, state, zip code

Ref: (Name of plan, IRA, etc.), (name of trustmaker), (account number)

Dear Sir/Madam:

I am the executor of the estate of (name of the trustmaker), who died on (date of death). (Name of trustmaker) was the owner of the above-referenced retirement account.

(Use one of the following paragraphs:)

Please forward all necessary forms and instructions for the beneficiaries to make their claims to me at the above address.

(or:)

Please forward all necessary forms and instructions to the beneficiary(ies) directly to the beneficiary(ies) as follows:

Name of beneficiary   (List each beneficiary)
Address of beneficiary
City, state, zip code
Social security number
Date of birth

Sincerely,

_____

(Your name), executor

Sample Checklist 11-9
LIST OF PENSIONS AND QUALIFIED PENSION PLAN
OF (NAME OF TRUSTMAKER)

Plan	Benefits available	Beneficiary
ABC Corporation	No	N/A
IRA, Trust Co. 1	Yes	Trust
IRA, Trust Co. 2	Yes	Jane Smith/John Jones
Savings plan	Yes	Estate

Checklist 11-10
PENSION OR OTHER QUALIFIED PENSION PLAN
AFTER DEATH OF TRUSTMAKER
Name of Plan _____

Action	Completed
1. Read the trust	
2. Read the will	
3. Determine beneficiary	
4. Coordinate with your tax advisor	
5. Contact plan administrator: a. Telephone	
b. Write letter (11-7 or 11-8)	
6. Receive required paperwork	
7. Submit paperwork	
8. Receive benefits	
9. Deposit benefits	

If the trust is the beneficiary of the pension plan, there will be tax consequences for the year the pension proceeds are received. The taxable portion of the pension is now subject to income tax as ordinary income. There is no spouse available to qualify for the tax-deferred basis of the plan.

Work with your tax advisor concerning the timing of receipt of the funds. Receipt in the year that you are distributing assets may be beneficial so that the tax consequences are shifted to the beneficiaries. You want to receive the funds in the year with the lowest taxable income.

Except for IRA's, there will be automatic withholding of federal income taxes. You may want to request withholding of state income taxes.

If the IRA or pension has named an individual as beneficiary, it would be wise to suggest that they contact their tax advisor concerning their options. They may have the option of receiving their benefits spread out over their expected lifetime rather than in one lump sum.

■ Other Death Benefits

The trustmaker may also have death benefits payable from an employer, labor union, or pension plan in addition to the pensions we just discussed. Check with these organizations to see if a death benefit is available. If so, request that the proper forms be sent to you.

Since there is no surviving spouse, the $255 social security death benefit is not available.

Checklist 11-11
OTHER POTENTIAL DEATH BENEFITS UPON
DEATH OF TRUSTMAKER

Action	Completed
1. Check with employer	
2. Check with union	
3. Check with pension	
4. Receive applicable forms	
5. Submit forms	
6. Receive benefits	
7. Deposit receipts	

■ Bank Accounts and Certificates of Deposit

Retitling accounts with banks, savings and loans, and credit unions is a relatively simple task. You are just changing the name of the trustee and probably the taxpayer ID number.

If the bank is local, it may be easiest to visit with them personally to request this change. If you prefer, you may use sample letter 11-9 to take care of it by mail.

Checklist 11-12
RETITLING BANK ACCOUNT(S) UPON DEATH OF TRUSTMAKER

Action	Completed
1. Read the trust	
2. Make list of all bank accounts	
3. Visit bank or write letter (11-11)	
4. Receive notification of change	

Sample Letter 11-9
RETITLING BANK ACCOUNT(S) UPON DEATH OF TRUSTMAKER

(Name of trust)
Your address
City, state, zip code

Date letter written

ABC Bank
Their address
Their city, state, zip code

Ref: Account (number)

Dear Sir/Madam:

I am the successor trustee of the (name of the trust) dated (date of the trust). The previous trustee, (name of previous trustmaker), died on (date of death). Please change the title of ownership for the above-referenced account(s) to:

(Your name), trustee
(Name of trust) dated (date of the original trust)
Trustee's address
Trustee's city, state, zip code

The taxpayer identification number for the trust is 12-3456789.

Enclosed are the following:

1. Form W-9
2. Certified copy of the death certificate of (name of deceased trustmaker)
3. (Appropriate pages of trust designating you as successor trustee).

If any additional forms are required, please send them to my address above.

Sincerely,

_____

(Your name), trustee

207

■ Personal Property

This should be an easy part of your job. There are no letters to write, and no transfer agents to contact. Since personal property is generally not titled in any owner's name, there is nothing that officially needs to be done.

Maintain a list of any significant items that you are managing as trustee, as well as the location where they are stored.

One area that you do need to check on is automobiles, boats, and other vehicles. Check with your local Department of Motor Vehicles to determine what needs to be done to allow you, as trustee, to control these assets.

Reporting to the Beneficiaries

One of the important jobs you have as trustee is to provide an accurate accounting to the beneficiaries. Unless directed otherwise by the terms of the trust, you will have to report periodically the results of your management efforts. Review the trust to determine how often reporting is required (usually annually or quarterly).

This should not be a difficult task, as you have been keeping separate records for the trust assets.

As a minimum you should provide:

1. Balance sheet

2. Profit-and-loss statement

3. A journal or ledger listing all transactions that occurred during the reporting period.

The formats for each of these reports will vary depending upon the assets owned by the trust. The main concept that you need to keep in mind is that these reports should be:

1. Accurate

2. Complete

3. Easy to understand

4. Timely

It is not possible in this book to cover all possible reporting situations that you may have to deal with. Check with your advisors to make sure that what you are doing is acceptable. Providing proper reports could very well keep you out of trouble down the line.

Here are some ideas that may help make this task easier for you as we discuss the various reports. You may develop your own methods that will meet the special needs of your trust.

■ Balance Sheet

This is nothing more than a listing of all the assets and liabilities of the trust. Depending on your desires, you may want to include values from previous periods for comparison.

If the trust includes assets that receive periodic statements, it may be helpful to attach these statements to the balance sheet. Example of this type of asset would include bank accounts, mutual funds, and stock brokerage accounts. The same is true if the trust owns real estate that is managed by a professional property manager.

An example of a balance sheet is given on page 210.

■ Profit-and-Loss Statement

This is simply a reporting of the trust's income and expenses for the reporting period. There may be very few entries or a large number, depending on the assets in the trust and the activity in the trust. This is basically the information you use to prepare the trust's tax returns (Form 1041).

An example of a simple profit-and-loss statement is given on page 211.

(Name of Trust)
BALANCE SHEET AS OF 12/31/XXXX

ASSETS

Cash	Current	Last Report
Bank of your town, checking	$ 547.50	$ 685.48
Certificate of deposit	4,544.80	4,415.95
Total Cash	$ 5,092.30	$ 5,101.43
Investments		
ABC mutual fund	14,945.88	12,153.19
Stock account — XYZ Mgmt.	347,940.44	365,288.14
Rental property — 125 Main	100,000.00	100,000.00
Total Investments	$462,886.32	$477,441.33
Total Assets	$467,978.62	$482,542.76

LIABILITIES

Current Liabilities		
Trustee fees	$ 500.00	$ 0.00
Long-term Liabilities		
Mortgage on rental	45,685.14	45,744.10
Total Liabilities	$46,185.14	$45,744.10
Net Worth	$421,793.48	$436,798.66

(Name of Trust)
PROFIT-AND-LOSS STATEMENT
1/1 – 12/31/XXXX

INCOME

Interest
Certificate of deposit $ 115.45

Dividends
ABC mutual fund   47.60
Managed stock account   12,491.15

Real estate
Rents   6,000.00
  Total Income $18,654.20

EXPENSES

Administrative
Trustee fees $1,000.00
Managed stock fees   6,958.82
Tax preparation   300.00
Total administrative expenses 8,258.82

Real estate
Property manager $ 600.00
Taxes   1,945.00
Insurance   650.00
Repairs   455.14
Depreciation   2,727.00
Total real estate expenses   6,377.14

  Total Expenses $14,635.96

  Net Profit $ 4,018.24

▪ Ledger/Journal

This is a reporting of all transactions, by date. For most trusts you can communicate all information needed in this area if you provide:

1. Checkbook register showing all cash deposits (including source) and all payments.

2. Copies of all mutual fund, stock brokerage, and savings account statements.

3. Copies of reports from real estate property managers.

These will provide a full, accurate reporting.

If your trust is fairly large or complex, you might consider using a fiduciary reporting software package which will provide you all of the necessary reports.

Check with your legal and accounting advisors to make sure that you are providing the necessary reports. The examples we used are very simple to show the format. Your advisors will show you what is necessary in your case and direct you to useful software if you need it.

PART 4

Transferring Assets Out of the Trust and Closing Down the Trust

CHAPTER 12

■ ■ ■ ■ ■ ■ ■ ■ ■

Transferring Assets From the Trust to the Beneficiaries

Up to now you have learned how to set up a trust, transfer assets to the trust, manage the trust, and transfer assets to different trusts. Now we will look at what you need to do when it is time to transfer assets to the beneficiaries.

The distribution area is often where the creator of the trust is the most creative. The primary purpose of most trusts is to provide for the orderly transfer of assets in the manner and form that suits the needs and desires of the trustmaker. As the trustee, you may find that certain transfers are required by the terms of the trust. Other transfers may be left to your discretion, if you are authorized by the trust document. Some may even be prohibited.

By now, I'm sure that you can see this coming. The first rule concerning transfers from the trust is that the trustee must READ THE TRUST.

As you read the trust, make a list of all allowable transfers. Include to whom the transfers are to be made, the frequency of the transfers, and any conditions that will trigger or block such a transfer. Indicate if the transfer is to be from the income of the trust, principal of the trust, or both.

Figure 12-1
TRANSFERS FROM TRUST B OF REVOCABLE LIVING
TRUST AFTER DEATH OF FIRST SPOUSE

Beneficiary	Surviving spouse	Surviving spouse	Surviving spouse
Amount	100% of income	Up to 5% of principal per year	As needed
Frequency	At least quarterly	As requested by spouse	As requested
Income/ Principal	Income	Principal	Principal
Triggered by	N/A	Surviving spouse's request	Emergency
Do not transfer if	N/A	N/A	Surviving spouse has remarried

Figure 12-2
TRANSFER FROM XYZ TRUST

Beneficiary	Child	Any child of trustmaker	Each child of trustmaker
Amount	⅓ of trust value	As needed	100% of trust divided evenly
Frequency	One time	As needed	One time
Income/ Principal	Either	Either	Both
Triggered by	Attains age 25	Child has college expenses	Death of both trustmakers
Do not transfer if	Cannot pass drug test	Child failed one or more courses last semester	Child is still a minor

An example of such a list, developed from Trust B of a revocable living trust after the death of the first spouse, is shown in Figure 12-1. Figure 12-2 gives an example of possible transfers from a trust other than the Trust B illustrated above.

Remember, both Figures 12-1 and 12-2 are simply examples of possible transfer situations and do not represent any specific trust. Read your trust to determine your transfer requirements.

If you are thinking of making a charitable gift from an irrevocable trust, make sure that the trust document allows such a gift. The trust may only make gifts to charities if the trustmaker specifically provided for them to be made. No matter how well-meaning your intentions are, you will be violating your fiduciary responsibilities if you make an unauthorized contribution to a charity. A second deterrent is that only authorized charitable gifts are deductible on your trust's income tax return.

Choosing the Method of Transfer

There are two basic ways that you can transfer assets from the trust. You can provide the beneficiary with cash, or you can transfer specific assets "in kind" by transferring the ownership of the assets to the beneficiary. As trustee, you must make the decision as to which method to use.

Like many of the other decisions you need to make while managing the trust, you must weigh various factors in making your decision. There will not always be an "ideal" solution.

Purpose of the Transfer

If the purpose of the transfer is to pay a beneficiary's bills, it would be logical to make the transfer in cash. On the other hand, if you transfer assets in the process of closing down the trust, it may be more appropriate to re-register the assets and transfer them "in kind" to the beneficiary.

The Beneficiaries' Needs, Wants, and Capabilities

You need to know your beneficiaries to make this decision. Check with each individual and explain that you can either sell or transfer various assets to them. Find out if there are any particular assets they want or do not want to receive. Try to determine if they have the capability of managing the various assets if they are transferred "in kind" to them.

Fair Division of Assets

If the trust is being divided between two or more beneficiaries, you must make sure that each receives his or her own fair share. As trustee, you may decide that it is best to cash out all assets and provide each beneficiary with their proportionate share of the cash. Or you may feel that an equal division of each asset may be the best way to do it. These choices could cause the most difficulties if you are not careful, particularly if there is any ill will among the beneficiaries.

Ease of Transfer

Some assets, such as mutual funds, are easy to divide and re-register to different beneficiaries. Other assets, such as real estate, a business, or a piece of art, may be difficult to either split or transfer. It may delay the transfer and the termination of the trust if you have to sell the asset first before distributing the cash.

Tax Considerations

Don't forget your silent partner in the trust, the Internal Revenue Service. The sale of any asset in order to provide a cash distribution is a taxable event. It could cause either a capital gain or a capital loss. The transfer of an asset to the beneficiary normally will not be considered a sale. Let's look at the various possibilities.

1. *Direct transfer of an asset to a beneficiary.* There would be no immediate tax consequences. The beneficiary would receive the asset with the same tax cost basis as the asset had within the

trust. The beneficiary would eventually be responsible for any capital gains or losses when they dispose of the asset in the future. The tax liability on any gain that was built up within the trust will have been shifted to the beneficiary.

2. *Sale of asset and trust not terminated in year of sale.* As you will recall from Chapter 7, trusts generally pass on the tax consequences to the beneficiaries for any income that is distributed to them. Capital gains are tax consequences that are not normally considered income and not passed on to beneficiaries. The trust will pay the capital gains taxes, and the cash received by the beneficiaries will not be subject directly to the capital gains taxes. Due to the taxes being paid, the distributions will probably be reduced.

3. *Sale of asset and trust terminated in the year of sale.* Capital gains are handled differently in the final year of operation of the trust. Since the trust is terminated by the end of the year, all income tax consequences are passed on to the beneficiaries. Capital gains and losses are included in each beneficiary's year-end Schedule K-1 and reported on their personal tax returns.

Your decision must weigh these factors in order to determine the best results for your beneficiaries.

Transferring Cash

Transferring cash is easy. When you receive the proceeds from the sale or as income from an investment of an asset, deposit it into the bank account or money market fund that you have established for the trust. Write the check to the beneficiary and you have completed your task.

Transferring Assets In Kind

The concept for these transfers should be very familiar to you. There is not much difference in the procedures for transferring assets out of the trust and transferring them into the trust. You will use basically the same letters, with some modifications to fit the circumstances.

Sample letters are provided shortly. Modify these letters to meet your situation. You may be transferring 100% or a portion of an asset to one beneficiary. Another situation will call for either an equal or unequal split of an asset among two or more beneficiaries. If you follow the models, you should have no difficulty in writing the letters to meet your needs.

There are a few things you need to keep in mind at this point. The first involves transfer of assets to a minor. Securities laws do not allow minors to own securities such as stocks, bonds, mutual funds, and limited partnerships. You will need to set up a custodial account under the Uniform Transfer to Minors Act for each child involved. Each custodial account must have one adult as the custodian. The custodian will be responsible for the management of the securities until the minor becomes an adult. The social security number for each account will be the minor's social security number. You would direct the assets to be registered as follows:

John Smith, custodian for:

James Smith under the (name of state) Uniform Transfer to Minors Act

(Address for the account)

Social security number: (minor's social security number)

Be sure to find out from each beneficiary how he or she wants the new account to be titled. Married individuals may desire that their share be maintained as separate property and registered in one name only. As an alternative, they may want to add their spouse to the title and hold the property as joint tenants or as community property. The beneficiary may have a trust and request that the asset be transferred directly to the trust. Check with your beneficiaries and get the correct information. It is just as easy to make the transfer to one of these entities as it is to the individual beneficiary.

When you enclose the appropriate pages from the trust, be sure to include the pages that name you as the trustee or successor trustee, as well as the front page, the signature page, and the pages naming the beneficiaries. Transfer companies always want to make sure that they are making the correct transfer.

If the transfers are a result of the death of one or more of the trustmakers, include this fact in your letter and attach a certified copy of the death certificate and a notarized affidavit of domicile.

Transferring Mutual Funds, Managed Accounts, Brokerage Accounts, and Limited Partnerships

The transfer of these investments will be handled in the same manner as transferring them into the trust. Usually a simple letter to the transfer agent or company is all that is necessary. Occasionally, the company will require their own paperwork, and limited partnerships usually have their own transfer forms.

Follow sample letter 12-1 to get the process started, and adjust it to meet your circumstances.

Transferring Individual Stock/Bond Certificates

Hopefully, by this time, you have learned the benefits of maintaining your stock and bond certificates in a brokerage account. If you still have individual stock and bond certificates, you will have to follow the same procedure that was used to transfer them into the trust. If you are splitting these certificates between more than one beneficiary, remember that they cannot be split into fractional shares. You will have to decide how to prorate an unequal division.

Sample letter 12-2 gives you the format to complete this transfer. You should have the name and address of the transfer agent and CUSIP number in your files from the time the certificates were transferred into the trust. If you don't, review Chapter 5 for details.

Sample Letter 12-1
TRANSFER TRUST ASSETS TO BENEFICIARY(IES) —
MUTUAL FUNDS, MANAGED ACCOUNTS, BROKERAGE
ACCOUNTS, LIMITED PARTNERSHIPS

(Name of trust)
Your street address
City, state, zip code

Date letter written

(Mutual fund family, stock brokerage, etc.)
Their address
Their city, state, zip code

Ref: (Name of investment) (account number) — (could be more
than one if in same mutual fund/limited partnership family)

Dear Sir/Madam:

I am the trustee of the (name of trust) dated (date of trust). In
accordance with the terms of the trust, I request that (100% of ____
shares [or] ____%) of the above-referenced account be re-registered
as follows:

> (Number of shares) (% of account, if more than one beneficiary)
> (New registration of account)
> Address   *(Same information for*
> City, state, zip code   *each beneficiary)*
> (Social security number [or] taxpayer ID number)

Enclosed are the following:

1. W-9 Form(s) (for each account)
2. Certified copy of death certificate of (trustmaker) (if appropriate)
3. Notarized affidavit of domicile (if appropriate).

(For limited partnerships, if transfer due to death of trustmaker, add
this paragraph:)

I understand that since this transfer is due to a death of an owner,
there is no transfer fee involved in this transaction.

Sincerely,

_____

(Your name), trustee

---

* Have signature Medallion-guaranteed.

Checklist 12-1

TRANSFER ASSETS OUT OF TRUST — MUTUAL FUNDS, MANAGED ACCOUNTS, BROKERAGE ACCOUNTS, LIMITED PARTNERSHIPS

Name of Asset _____

Action	Completed
1. Read the trust	
2. Verify transfer is authorized	
3. Verify beneficiary's preferred titling	
4. Write letter (12-1)	
5. Obtain w-9's from beneficiaries	
6. Notarize affidavit	
7. Sign letter (signature guaranteed)	
8. Complete any follow-up paperwork	
9. Receive acknowledgment of completed transfer	

Sample Letter 12-2
TRANSFER TRUST ASSETS TO BENEFICIARY(IES) — INDIVIDUAL STOCK AND BOND CERTIFICATES

Name of trust
Your street address
City, state, zip code

Date letter written

Transfer agent
Their address
Their city, state, zip code

Ref: (Name of corporation) (CUSIP number) (number of shares) (certificate numbers)

Dear Sir/Madam:

I am the trustee of the (name of trust) dated (date of trust). In accordance with the terms of the trust, I request that the above-referenced certificate(s) be re-registered as follows:

(Number of shares, if more than one beneficiary)
(New registration of account)
Address   *(Same information for*
City, state, zip code   *each beneficiary)*
(Social security number [or] taxpayer ID number)

Please forward the new certificates directly to each new owner.

Enclosed are the following:

1. W-9 Form(s) (for each beneficiary)
2. Certified copy of death certificate of (trustmaker) (if appropriate)
3. Notarized affidavit of domicile (if appropriate)
4. Stock/bond powers (if used).

Sincerely,

_____

(Your name), trustee

* Have signature Medallion-guaranteed.

Checklist 12-2
TRANSFER ASSETS OUT OF TRUST —
STOCK/BOND CERTIFICATES
Name of Stock/Bond_____

Action	Completed
1. Read the trust	
2. Verify transfer is authorized	
3. Certificate bond	
4. Verify beneficiaries' preferred titling	
5. Write letter (12-2)	
6. Obtain w-9's from beneficiary	
7. Sign letter (signature guaranteed)	
8. Sign stock certificate/bond/stock power (signature guaranteed)	
9. Notarize affidavit of domicile	
10. Mail letter by insured U.S. Mail	
11. Verify beneficiaries receive new certificates/bonds	

Lost Stock Certificate/Bond

After all of the work you have done to transfer these certificates in the past, let's assume that you have maintained your certificate in a safe place and that they are not lost. If by some remote chance you have misplaced any certificates, follow the same procedures set forth in Chapter 5 to have replacements issued.

Real Estate

To transfer real estate, you need to prepare a deed transferring the property from the trust to the beneficiary. Check with your attorney to determine the proper type of deed to use. Different states require different types of deeds. You must have your signature notarized. Also, check with your attorney or the County Recorder's office to make sure that all other documents (such as death certificates) necessary to clear the title are recorded at the same time you record the deed that transfers the property.

Checklist 12-3
TRANSFER ASSETS OUT OF TRUST — REAL ESTATE
Name of Property _____

Action	Completed
1. Read the trust	
2. Verify transfer is authorized	
3. Verify beneficiary's preferred titling	
4. Consult with attorney as to proper form for deed	
5. Prepare deed	
6. Have your signature on deed notarized	
7. Record deed at County Recorder's office	

Personal Property

Personal property items such as jewelry, furniture, collectibles and clothing do not have titles recorded by an outside party. My recommendation is to prepare a list of assets, or *inventory*, of any of these items that are given to the beneficiary. Have the beneficiary acknowledge receipt of these items by signing the inventory. Return the signed inventory list to the trust records.

Checklist 12-4
TRANSFER ASSETS OUT OF TRUST — PERSONAL PROPERTY

Action	Completed
1. Read the trust	
2. Verify transfer is authorized	
3. Prepare inventory for each beneficiary	
4. Have each beneficiary sign inventory acknowledging receipt	

Automobiles and Other Vehicles

Motor vehicles such as automobiles, boats, motorcycles, and trucks are registered with the state Department of Motor Vehicles. Many larger boats are instead registered with the federal government. In order to transfer ownership, contact the appropriate registration agency, obtain the proper paperwork, and submit your completed paperwork to the proper office.

CHAPTER 13

■ ■ ■ ■ ■ ■ ■ ■ ■

Terminating The Trust

It is said that the two happiest days in a boat owner's life are the day the boat is first purchased and the day that it is sold. Perhaps you'll agree that the happiest day in a trustee's life is the day that the trust completes its operations.

After using the earlier sections of this book, you should find this last function of the trustee to be very simple and logical. There are three basic steps involved:

1. Transfer all assets to the beneficiaries.
2. File the final tax returns.
3. Provide a final accounting to the beneficiaries.

Transfer All Assets to the Beneficiaries

As you prepare to transfer the assets out of the trust to the beneficiaries, you have to decide whether to sell the assets and distribute the cash proceeds or to transfer the assets directly to the beneficiaries. Your decision will be based upon:

1. The terms of the trust
2. The desires of the beneficiaries
3. Your perception of the management capabilities of the beneficiaries
4. The ease of division of the various assets if there are multiple beneficiaries
5. The costs involved in either liquidating or transferring the assets directly

6. The tax consequences of a sale of the asset

If you need some assistance with making these decisions, contact your advisors. They may give you insights that make your choices obvious.

Review the sample letters and checklists in Chapter 12 to make the actual transfers to the beneficiaries.

If at all possible, start your transfer-out procedures in time to have all transfers completed before the end of December. This way you will be able to close out the trust without having to carry it forward through another tax year.

Final Tax Return

The final income tax return for the trust (Form 1041) will be very similar to the previous returns you have filed for the trust. This chapter discusses only the differences; review Chapter 7 for other details.

Be sure to check the box near the top of Form 1041 indicates this is a "Final Return." This will prevent the Internal Revenue Service from looking for returns in future years. It's much easier to check this block than to answer an inquiry a few years later as to where is the tax return for a later year.

The other differences will be on Schedule K-1, which reports the beneficiaries' share of income and deductions. Since all of the assets have been distributed in the current year, all of the income will probably be reported on the Schedule K-1's to be included on the beneficiaries' personal returns. It is very unlikely that the trust will earn more income than the total amount of assets that are distributed.

Final K-1

Be sure to mark the box at the top of the K-1 that indicates "Final K-1." This will allow the beneficiaries the opportunity to deduct any passive losses that are indicated on the lines directing reporting on Schedule E of Form 1040.

Excess Deductions On Termination

There are some different lines that can be used on the final K-1's. They are found in the section titled "Deductions in the final year of trust or decedent's estate." The first is "Excess deductions on termination." These excess deductions occur when the total deductions for the trust, excluding the charitable deduction and exemption, are greater than the gross income during the final tax year.

Only the beneficiaries who receive the trust's assets are allowed to benefit from the excess deductions. If a beneficiary doesn't have enough income on his or her personal tax return to absorb this excess deduction, it cannot be carried forward to future years. An individual beneficiary uses the deduction as part of the miscellaneous deductions on Schedule A that are subject to the 2% of adjusted gross income limitations. The deduction is not useful if the beneficiary does not itemize deductions.

Capital Loss Carryovers

Up until the final year of the trust, all capital gains and losses generally remain with the trust. In the final year, any capital gains are reported to the beneficiaries as income. Also, capital losses that have not been used by the trust are now distributed to the beneficiaries for use on their own tax returns. These losses are used on Schedule D by each beneficiary and can be carried forward until used up.

Net Operating Losses

In addition to the excess deductions, any net operating losses for the trust's business activities are also distributed to the beneficiaries for use on their own returns. These can be used even if the beneficiary doesn't itemize their deductions.

Form 56

Add one more item to your final trust tax return. Form 56, which you used to report your fiduciary responsibility to the IRS, can now be used to terminate your responsibility.

Final Accounting to Beneficiaries

Once all assets have been transferred to the beneficiaries and the final tax returns have been filed, it is time to complete your job. Make a final set of reports to the beneficiaries using the same formats that you used while operating the trust.

As part of the final accounting, provide the beneficiaries with the tax cost basis of all assets that you transferred directly to them. This will greatly ease their tax reporting in the future when they sell the assets. It will also save you from having to look this information up for them later.

Checklist 13-1

TERMINATING THE TRUST

Action	Completed
1. Read the trust	
2. Prepare list of assets	
3. Determine which assets to sell and which to transfer in kind to beneficiaries	
4. Determine split of assets	
5. Sell appropriate assets	
6. Transfer assets to beneficiaries	
7. Prepare final tax returns	
8. Mail returns	
9. Provide beneficiaries with K-1's	
10. Make final accounting report to beneficiaries	
11. Report cost basis of assets to beneficiaries	
12. Enjoy well-deserved rest	

Checklist 13-2
LIST OF ASSETS TO TERMINATE THE TRUST

Name of asset	To which beneficiary	Sell	Transfer	Completed

CHAPTER 14

■ ■ ■ ■ ■ ■ ■ ■ ■

Just Do It!

More problems in life are caused by inaction than by action. Most inaction is caused by lack of knowledge. When we don't understand something, we tend to shy away from it. We'll do as many other tasks as we can while putting aside what we are unsure about. Maybe it will just take care of itself!

The above is true when it comes to properly acting as a trustee of a trust. It's easy to delay until "later" making the proper transfers, contacting the beneficiaries, or whatever the task may be.

Now you have no excuse. Your tasks have been outlined, and the samples have done a lot of the work for you. You understand how a trust operates and what you need to do. *The Truth About Trusts* has made your job easy.

Remember, you are not alone as you tackle this important task of being a trustee. Rely on the assistance of your coaches—your advisors. They have probably been down this path many times with their other clients. Use them: they'll keep you out of trouble. You'll find it much easier and less costly to get help to do the job right in the first place than to correct errors later.

I wish you luck as you move forward and reap the rewards offered by your trust. Allow me to leave you with a brief tale that I heard many years ago and often use to close my seminars.

Three men were riding their camels across the desert on a hot afternoon. All of the sudden, out of the heavens, a deep booming voice called out, "Stop your camels." They stopped, looked around, but saw no one. Next, the voice said, "Get down off your camels." By this time they were getting a little worried, so they obeyed. A third time the voice was heard. This time it said, "Reach down, pick up some pebbles, and put them in your pocket." This really puzzled them, but they followed the directions. Then the voice gave one last command, "Stay here tonight, and tomorrow you will be both happy and sad."

The three men were thoroughly confused, but decided that they had better do what the voice said. They stayed the night. The next morning as they were packing their camels, one of the men reached into his pocket. When he pulled out the pebbles, he found to his delight that they had all turned to gemstones—diamonds, rubies, emeralds, and sapphires. Upon seeing the excitement of the man, the others also reached into their pockets. They had the same results.

Then one of them realized what the voice had meant. They were happy that they had picked up the pebbles, but sad that they had not picked up more of them.

My sincere wish to you is that by reading *The Truth About Trusts,* you have picked up some pebbles that will turn into gemstones for you. You have one major advantage over the three men riding their camels. They were unable to go back and pick up more pebbles. You can go back as many times as you want. You can re-read parts of this book and continue to pick up more pebbles. However, your pebbles will only turn into gemstones if you put the ideas that you have learned to work.

As the shoe company's slogan says, "Just do it."

sample forms

FORM SS-4

Form **SS-4**
(Rev. February 1998)
Department of the Treasury
Internal Revenue Service

Application for Employer Identification Number

(For use by employers, corporations, partnerships, trusts, estates, churches, government agencies, certain individuals, and others. See instructions.)

► **Keep a copy for your records.**

EIN

OMB No. 1545-0003

Please type or print clearly.

1 Name of applicant (legal name) (see instructions)

2 Trade name of business (if different from name on line 1)

3 Executor, trustee, "care of" name

4a Mailing address (street address) (room, apt., or suite no.)

5a Business address (if different from address on lines 4a and 4b)

4b City, state, and ZIP code

5b City, state, and ZIP code

6 County and state where principal business is located

7 Name of principal officer, general partner, grantor, owner, or trustor—SSN or ITIN may be required (see instructions) ►

8a Type of entity (Check only one box.) (see instructions)
Caution: *If applicant is a limited liability company, see the instructions for line 8a.*

☐ Sole proprietor (SSN)
☐ Partnership
☐ REMIC
☐ State/local government
☐ Church or church-controlled organization
☐ Other nonprofit organization (specify) ► (enter GEN if applicable)
☐ Other (specify) ►
☐ Personal service corp.
☐ National Guard
☐ Farmers' cooperative
☐ Estate (SSN of decedent)
☐ Plan administrator (SSN)
☐ Other corporation (specify) ►
☐ Trust
☐ Federal government/military

8b If a corporation, name the state or foreign country (if applicable) where incorporated — State — Foreign country

9 Reason for applying (Check only one box.) (see instructions)
☐ Started new business (specify type) ►
☐ Hired employees (Check the box and see line 12.)
☐ Created a pension plan (specify type) ►
☐ Banking purpose (specify purpose) ►
☐ Changed type of organization (specify new type) ►
☐ Purchased going business
☐ Created a trust (specify type) ►
☐ Other (specify) ►

10 Date business started or acquired (month, day, year) (see instructions)

11 Closing month of accounting year (see instructions)

12 First date wages or annuities were paid or will be paid (month, day, year). **Note:** *If applicant is a withholding agent, enter date income will first be paid to nonresident alien. (month, day, year)* . . . . ►

13 Highest number of employees expected in the next 12 months. **Note:** *If the applicant does not expect to have any employees during the period, enter -0-. (see instructions)* . . . . ►

Nonagricultural	Agricultural	Household

14 Principal activity (see instructions) ►

15 Is the principal business activity manufacturing? . . . . ☐ **Yes** ☐ **No**
If "Yes," principal product and raw material used ►

16 To whom are most of the products or services sold? Please check one box. ☐ Business (wholesale)
☐ Public (retail) ☐ Other (specify) ► ☐ N/A

17a Has the applicant ever applied for an employer identification number for this or any other business? . . . . ☐ **Yes** ☐ **No**
Note: *If "Yes," please complete lines 17b and 17c.*

17b If you checked "Yes" on line 17a, give applicant's legal name and trade name shown on prior application, if different from line 1 or 2 above.
Legal name ► Trade name ►

17c Approximate date when and city and state where the application was filed. Enter previous employer identification number if known.

Approximate date when filed (mo., day, year)	City and state where filed	Previous EIN

Under penalties of perjury, I declare that I have examined this application, and to the best of my knowledge and belief, it is true, correct, and complete.

Business telephone number (include area code)

Fax telephone number (include area code)

Name and title (Please type or print clearly.) ►

Signature ► Date ►

Note: *Do not write below this line. For official use only.*

Please leave blank ►	Geo.	Ind.	Class	Size	Reason for applying

For Paperwork Reduction Act Notice, see page 4. Cat. No. 16055N Form **SS-4** (Rev. 2-98)

FORM 56

Form **56** (Rev. August 1997) Department of the Treasury Internal Revenue Service	**Notice Concerning Fiduciary Relationship** (Internal Revenue Code sections 6036 and 6903)	OMB No. 1545-0013

Part I   Identification

Name of person for whom you are acting (as shown on the tax return)	Identifying number	Decedent's social security no.

Address of person for whom you are acting (number, street, and room or suite no.)

City or town, state, and ZIP code (If a foreign address, see instructions.)

Fiduciary's name

Address of fiduciary (number, street, and room or suite no.)

City or town, state, and ZIP code	Telephone number (optional) ( )

Part II   Authority

1   Authority for fiduciary relationship. Check applicable box:

a(1) ☐ Will and codicils or court order appointing fiduciary. Attach certified copy . .   **(2)** Date of death ....

b(1) ☐ Court order appointing fiduciary. Attach certified copy . . . .   **(2)** Date (see instructions) ....

c   ☐ Valid trust instrument and amendments. Attach copy

d   ☐ Other. Describe ▶ ....

Part III   Tax Notices

Send to the fiduciary listed in Part I all notices and other written communications involving the following tax matters:

2   Type of tax (estate, gift, generation-skipping transfer, income, excise, etc.) ▶ ....

3   Federal tax form number (706, 1040, 1041, 1120, etc.) ▶ ....

4   Year(s) or period(s) (if estate tax, date of death) ▶ ....

Part IV   Revocation or Termination of Notice

Section A—Total Revocation or Termination

5   Check this box if you are revoking or terminating all prior notices concerning fiduciary relationships on file with the Internal
Revenue Service for the same tax matters and years or periods covered by this notice concerning fiduciary relationship . ▶ ☐
Reason for termination of fiduciary relationship. Check applicable box:

a   ☐ Court order revoking fiduciary authority. Attach certified copy.

b   ☐ Certificate of dissolution or termination of a business entity. Attach copy.

c   ☐ Other. Describe ▶

Section B—Partial Revocation

6a   Check this box if you are revoking earlier notices concerning fiduciary relationships on file with the Internal Revenue Service for
the same tax matters and years or periods covered by this notice concerning fiduciary relationship . . . . ▶ ☐

b   Specify to whom granted, date, and address, including ZIP code, or refer to attached copies of earlier notices and authorizations
▶ ....

Section C—Substitute Fiduciary

7   Check this box if a new fiduciary or fiduciaries have been or will be substituted for the revoking or terminating fiduciary(ies) and
specify the name(s) and address(es), including ZIP code(s), of the new fiduciary(ies) . . . . ▶ ☐

Part V   Court and Administrative Proceedings

Name of court (if other than a court proceeding, identify the type of proceeding and name of agency)	Date proceeding initiated	
Address of court	Docket number of proceeding	
City or town, state, and ZIP code	Date Time a.m. p.m.	Place of other proceedings

I certify that I have the authority to execute this notice concerning fiduciary relationship on behalf of the taxpayer.

Please Sign Here	Fiduciary's signature	Title, if applicable	Date
	Fiduciary's signature	Title, if applicable	Date

For Paperwork Reduction Act and Privacy Act Notice, see back page.   Cat. No. 16375I   Form **56** (Rev. 8-97)

FORM W-9

Form **W-9** (Rev. December 1996) Department of the Treasury Internal Revenue Service	**Request for Taxpayer Identification Number and Certification**	Give form to the requester. Do NOT send to the IRS.

Name (If a joint account or you changed your name, see **Specific Instructions** on page 2.)

Business name, if different from above. (See **Specific Instructions** on page 2.)

Check appropriate box: ☐ Individual/Sole proprietor ☐ Corporation ☐ Partnership ☐ Other ▶ ....

Address (number, street, and apt. or suite no.) | Requester's name and address (optional)

City, state, and ZIP code

Part I Taxpayer Identification Number (TIN) | List account number(s) here (optional)

Enter your TIN in the appropriate box. For individuals, this is your social security number (SSN). However, if you are a resident alien OR a sole proprietor, see the instructions on page 2. For other entities, it is your employer identification number (EIN). If you do not have a number, see **How To Get a TIN** on page 2.

Social security number

OR

Employer identification number

Note: *If the account is in more than one name, see the chart on page 2 for guidelines on whose number to enter.*

Part II For Payees Exempt From Backup Withholding (See the instructions on page 2.) ▶

Part III Certification

Under penalties of perjury, I certify that:

1. The number shown on this form is my correct taxpayer identification number (or I am waiting for a number to be issued to me), **and**

2. I am not subject to backup withholding because: **(a)** I am exempt from backup withholding, or **(b)** I have not been notified by the Internal Revenue Service (IRS) that I am subject to backup withholding as a result of a failure to report all interest or dividends, or **(c)** the IRS has notified me that I am no longer subject to backup withholding.

Certification Instructions.—You must cross out item **2** above if you have been notified by the IRS that you are currently subject to backup withholding because you have failed to report all interest and dividends on your tax return. For real estate transactions, item **2** does not apply. For mortgage interest paid, acquisition or abandonment of secured property, cancellation of debt, contributions to an individual retirement arrangement (IRA), and generally, payments other than interest and dividends, you are not required to sign the Certification, but you must provide your correct TIN. (See the instructions on page 2.)

Sign Here | Signature ▶ | Date ▶

STOCK/BOND POWER

ACCOUNT NO. _____ _____

IRREVOCABLE STOCK OR BOND POWER

For Value Received, the undersigned does (do) hereby sell, assign and transfer to

_____
NAME OF TRANSFEREE   SOCIAL SECURITY NUMBER OR TAX ID

FOR STOCK:

_____ shares of the common/preferred stock of _____

represented by Certificate(s) No(s). _____inclusive,

standing in the name of the undersigned on the books of said Company.

FOR BONDS:

_____ bonds of _____

in the principal amount of $ _____, No.(s). _____

inclusive, standing in the name of the undersigned on the books of said Company.

The undersigned does (do) hereby irrevocably constitute and appoint

_____ attorney to transfer the said stock or bond(s), as the case may be,

on the books of said Company, with full power of substitution in the premises.

Signature _____

Dated _____ **Signature** _____

SIGNATURE(S) GUARANTEE:

239

FORM 1041

Form 1041

Department of the Treasury—Internal Revenue Service

U.S. Income Tax Return for Estates and Trusts

1998

For calendar year 1998 or fiscal year beginning , 1998, and ending , 19 | OMB No. 1545-0092

A Type of entity:	Name of estate or trust (If a grantor type trust, see page 8 of the instructions.)	C Employer identification number
☐ Decedent's estate		
☐ Simple trust		D Date entity created
☐ Complex trust	Name and title of fiduciary	E Nonexempt charitable and split-interest trusts, check applicable boxes (see page 10 of the instructions):
☐ Grantor type trust		
☐ Bankruptcy estate–Ch. 7		
☐ Bankruptcy estate–Ch. 11	Number, street, and room or suite no. (If a P.O. box, see page 8 of the instructions.)	
☐ Pooled income fund		☐ Described in section 4947(a)(1)
B Number of Schedules K-1 attached (see instructions) ▶	City or town, state, and ZIP code	☐ Not a private foundation
		☐ Described in section 4947(a)(2)

F Check applicable boxes:	☐ Initial return	☐ Final return	☐ Amended return	G Pooled mortgage account (see page 10 of the instructions):
	☐ Change in fiduciary's name	☐ Change in fiduciary's address		☐ Bought ☐ Sold Date:

Income

1	Interest income	**1**	
2	Ordinary dividends	**2**	
3	Business income or (loss) (attach Schedule C or C-EZ (Form 1040))	**3**	
4	Capital gain or (loss) (attach Schedule D (Form 1041))	**4**	
5	Rents, royalties, partnerships, other estates and trusts, etc. (attach Schedule E (Form 1040))	**5**	
6	Farm income or (loss) (attach Schedule F (Form 1040))	**6**	
7	Ordinary gain or (loss) (attach Form 4797)	**7**	
8	Other income. List type and amount	**8**	
9	**Total income.** Combine lines 1 through 8 . . . . ▶	**9**	

Deductions

10	Interest. Check if Form 4952 is attached ▶ ☐	**10**	
11	Taxes	**11**	
12	Fiduciary fees	**12**	
13	Charitable deduction (from Schedule A, line 7)	**13**	
14	Attorney, accountant, and return preparer fees	**14**	
15a	Other deductions NOT subject to the 2% floor (attach schedule)	**15a**	
b	Allowable miscellaneous itemized deductions subject to the 2% floor	**15b**	
16	**Total.** Add lines 10 through 15b . . . . ▶	**16**	
17	Adjusted total income or (loss). Subtract line 16 from line 9. Enter here and on Schedule B, line 1 ▶	**17**	
18	Income distribution deduction (from Schedule B, line 15) (attach Schedules K-1 (Form 1041))	**18**	
19	Estate tax deduction (including certain generation-skipping taxes) (attach computation) . .	**19**	
20	Exemption	**20**	
21	**Total deductions.** Add lines 18 through 20 . . . . ▶	**21**	

Tax and Payments

22	Taxable income. Subtract line 21 from line 17. If a loss, see page 14 of the instructions	**22**	
23	**Total tax** (from Schedule G, line 8)	**23**	
24	**Payments: a** 1998 estimated tax payments and amount applied from 1997 return . . .	**24a**	
b	Estimated tax payments allocated to beneficiaries (from Form 1041-T)	**24b**	
c	Subtract line 24b from line 24a	**24c**	
d	Tax paid with extension of time to file: ☐ Form 2758 ☐ Form 8736 ☐ Form 8800	**24d**	
e	Federal income tax withheld. If any is from Form(s) 1099, check ▶ ☐	**24e**	
	Other payments: **f** Form 2439 .... ; **g** Form 4136 .... ; Total ▶	**24h**	
25	**Total payments.** Add lines 24c through 24e, and 24h . . . . ▶	**25**	
26	Estimated tax penalty (see page 15 of the instructions)	**26**	
27	**Tax due.** If line 25 is smaller than the total of lines 23 and 26, enter amount owed . . .	**27**	
28	**Overpayment.** If line 25 is larger than the total of lines 23 and 26, enter amount overpaid	**28**	
29	Amount of line 28 to be: **a** Credited to 1999 estimated tax ▶ ; **b** Refunded ▶	**29**	

Please Sign Here

Under penalties of perjury, I declare that I have examined this return, including accompanying schedules and statements, and to the best of my knowledge and belief, it is true, correct, and complete. Declaration of preparer (other than fiduciary) is based on all information of which preparer has any knowledge.

▶		▶	
Signature of fiduciary or officer representing fiduciary	Date	EIN of fiduciary if a financial institution (see page 5 of the instructions)

Paid Preparer's Use Only

Preparer's signature ▶		Date		Check if self-employed ▶ ☐	Preparer's social security no.
Firm's name (or yours if self-employed) and address ▶				EIN ▶	
				ZIP code ▶	

For Paperwork Reduction Act Notice, see the separate instructions. | Cat. No. 11370H | Form **1041** (1998)

FORM 1041 – page 2

Form 1041 (1998) Page **2**

Schedule A — Charitable Deduction. Do not complete for a simple trust or a pooled income fund.

1	Amounts paid or permanently set aside for charitable purposes from gross income (see page 15)	1
2	Tax-exempt income allocable to charitable contributions (see page 16 of the instructions) . .	2
3	Subtract line 2 from line 1	3
4	Capital gains for the tax year allocated to corpus and paid or permanently set aside for charitable purposes	4
5	Add lines 3 and 4	5
6	Section 1202 exclusion allocable to capital gains paid or permanently set aside for charitable purposes (see page 16 of the instructions)	6
7	**Charitable deduction.** Subtract line 6 from 5. Enter here and on page 1, line 13	7

Schedule B — Income Distribution Deduction

1	Adjusted total income (from page 1, line 17) (see page 16 of the instructions)	1
2	Adjusted tax-exempt interest	2
3	Total net gain from Schedule D (Form 1041), line 16, column (1) (see page 16 of the instructions)	3
4	Enter amount from Schedule A, line 4 (reduced by any allocable section 1202 exclusion). . .	4
5	Capital gains for the tax year included on Schedule A, line 1 (see page 16 of the instructions)	5
6	Enter any gain from page 1, line 4, as a negative number. If page 1, line 4, is a loss, enter the loss as a positive number	6
7	**Distributable net income (DNI).** Combine lines 1 through 6. If zero or less, enter -0-. . . .	7
8	If a complex trust, enter accounting income for the tax year as determined under the governing instrument and applicable local law 8	
9	Income required to be distributed currently	9
10	Other amounts paid, credited, or otherwise required to be distributed	10
11	Total distributions. Add lines 9 and 10. If greater than line 8, see page 17 of the instructions	11
12	Enter the amount of tax-exempt income included on line 11	12
13	Tentative income distribution deduction. Subtract line 12 from line 11	13
14	Tentative income distribution deduction. Subtract line 2 from line 7. If zero or less, enter -0-	14
15	Income distribution deduction. Enter the smaller of line 13 or line 14 here and on page 1, line 18	15

Schedule G — Tax Computation (see page 17 of the instructions)

1	**Tax: a** ☐ Tax rate schedule or ☐ Schedule D (Form 1041) . .	1a
	b Tax on lump-sum distributions (attach Form 4972). . . .	1b
	c Total. Add lines 1a and 1b. . . . . ▶	1c
2a	Foreign tax credit (attach Form 1116)	2a
b	Check: ☐ Nonconventional source fuel credit ☐ Form 8834 . . .	2b
c	General business credit. Enter here and check which forms are attached: ☐ Form 3800 or ☐ Forms (specify) ▶............................	2c
d	Credit for prior year minimum tax (attach Form 8801)	2d
3	**Total credits.** Add lines 2a through 2d . . . . ▶	3
4	Subtract line 3 from line 1c	4
5	Recapture taxes. Check if from: ☐ Form 4255 ☐ Form 8611.	5
6	Alternative minimum tax (from Schedule I, line 39).	6
7	Household employment taxes. Attach Schedule H (Form 1040)	7
8	**Total tax.** Add lines 4 through 7. Enter here and on page 1, line 23 . . . . ▶	8

Other Information

		Yes	No
1	Did the estate or trust receive tax-exempt income? If "Yes," attach a computation of the allocation of expenses. Enter the amount of tax-exempt interest income and exempt-interest dividends ▶ $		
2	Did the estate or trust receive all or any part of the earnings (salary, wages, and other compensation) of any individual by reason of a contract assignment or similar arrangement?		
3	At any time during calendar year 1998, did the estate or trust have an interest in or a signature or other authority over a bank, securities, or other financial account in a foreign country? See page 19 of the instructions for exceptions and filing requirements for Form TD F 90-22.1. If "Yes," enter the name of the foreign country ▶		
4	During the tax year, did the estate or trust receive a distribution from, or was it the grantor of, or transferor to, a foreign trust? If "Yes," the estate or trust may have to file Form 3520. See page 19 of the instructions . . .		
5	Did the estate or trust receive, or pay, any seller-financed mortgage interest? If "Yes," see page 19 for required attachment .		
6	If this is an estate or a complex trust making the section 663(b) election, check here (see page 19) . . ▶ ☐		
7	To make a section 643(e)(3) election, attach Schedule D (Form 1041), and check here (see page 19). . ▶ ☐		
8	If the decedent's estate has been open for more than 2 years, attach an explanation for the delay in closing the estate, and check here ▶ ☐		
9	Are any present or future trust beneficiaries skip persons? See page 19 of the instructions		

FORM 1041 – page 3

Form 1041 (1998)   Page 3

Schedule I **Alternative Minimum Tax** (see pages 19 through 24 of the instructions)

Part I—Estate's or Trust's Share of Alternative Minimum Taxable Income

1	Adjusted total income or (loss) (from page 1, line 17).	**1**	
2	Net operating loss deduction. Enter as a positive amount	**2**	
3	Add lines 1 and 2	**3**	
4	**Adjustments and tax preference items:**		
a	Interest	**4a**	
b	Taxes	**4b**	
c	Miscellaneous itemized deductions (from page 1, line 15b).	**4c**	
d	Refund of taxes	**4d** ( )	
e	Depreciation of property placed in service after 1986	**4e**	
f	Circulation and research and experimental expenditures	**4f**	
g	Mining exploration and development costs	**4g**	
h	Long-term contracts entered into after February 28, 1986	**4h**	
i	Amortization of pollution control facilities	**4i**	
j	Installment sales of certain property	**4j**	
k	Adjusted gain or loss (including incentive stock options).	**4k**	
l	Certain loss limitations	**4l**	
m	Tax shelter farm activities	**4m**	
n	Passive activities	**4n**	
o	Beneficiaries of other trusts or decedent's estates	**4o**	
p	Tax-exempt interest from specified private activity bonds	**4p**	
q	Depletion	**4q**	
r	Accelerated depreciation of real property placed in service before 1987	**4r**	
s	Accelerated depreciation of leased personal property placed in service before 1987	**4s**	
t	Intangible drilling costs	**4t**	
u	Other adjustments	**4u**	
5	Combine lines 4a through 4u.	**5**	
6	Add lines 3 and 5	**6**	
7	Alternative tax net operating loss deduction (see page 23 of the instructions for limitations).	**7**	
8	Adjusted alternative minimum taxable income. Subtract line 7 from line 6. Enter here and on line 13	**8**	
	Note: *Complete Part II below before going to line 9.*		
9	Income distribution deduction from line 27 below	**9**	
10	Estate tax deduction (from page 1, line 19)	**10**	
11	Add lines 9 and 10	**11**	
12	Estate's or trust's share of alternative minimum taxable income. Subtract line 11 from line 8 .	**12**	

If line 12 is:
- $22,500 or less, stop here and enter -0- on Schedule G, line 6. The estate or trust is not liable for the alternative minimum tax.
- Over $22,500, but less than $165,000, go to line 28.
- $165,000 or more, enter the amount from line 12 on line 34 and go to line 35.

Part II—Income Distribution Deduction on a Minimum Tax Basis

13	Adjusted alternative minimum taxable income (from line 8)	**13**	
14	Adjusted tax-exempt interest (other than amounts included on line 4p)	**14**	
15	Total net gain from Schedule D (Form 1041), line 16, column (1). If a loss, enter -0-	**15**	
16	Capital gains for the tax year allocated to corpus and paid or permanently set aside for charitable purposes (from Schedule A, line 4)	**16**	
17	Capital gains paid or permanently set aside for charitable purposes from gross income (see page 23 of the instructions)	**17**	
18	Capital gains computed on a minimum tax basis included on line 8	**18** ( )	
19	Capital losses computed on a minimum tax basis included on line 8. Enter as a positive amount	**19**	
20	Distributable net alternative minimum taxable income (DNAMTI). Combine lines 13 through 19. If zero or less, enter -0-	**20**	
21	Income required to be distributed currently (from Schedule B, line 9)	**21**	
22	Other amounts paid, credited, or otherwise required to be distributed (from Schedule B, line 10)	**22**	
23	Total distributions. Add lines 21 and 22	**23**	
24	Tax-exempt income included on line 23 (other than amounts included on line 4p)	**24**	
25	Tentative income distribution deduction on a minimum tax basis. Subtract line 24 from line 23.	**25**	
26	Tentative income distribution deduction on a minimum tax basis. Subtract line 14 from line 20. If zero or less, enter -0-	**26**	
27	**Income distribution deduction on a minimum tax basis.** Enter the smaller of line 25 or line 26. Enter here and on line 9	**27**	

FORM 1041 – page 4

Form 1041 (1998)
Page **4**

Part III—Alternative Minimum Tax

28	Exemption amount	28	$22,500
29	Enter the amount from line 12	29	
30	Phase-out of exemption amount	30	$75,000
31	Subtract line 30 from line 29. If zero or less, enter -0-	31	
32	Multiply line 31 by 25% (.25).	32	
33	Subtract line 32 from line 28. If zero or less, enter -0-	33	
34	Subtract line 33 from line 29	34	

35 If the estate or trust completed Schedule D (Form 1041) and has an amount on line 24 or 26 (or would have had an amount on either line if Part V had been completed) (as refigured for the AMT, if necessary), go to Part IV below to figure line 35. **All others:** If line 34 is—
 • $175,000 or less, multiply line 34 by 26% (.26).
 • Over $175,000, multiply line 34 by 28% (.28) and subtract $3,500 from the result . . . . | 35 |

36	Alternative minimum foreign tax credit (see page 23 of instructions)	36	
37	Tentative minimum tax. Subtract line 36 from line 35	37	
38	Enter the tax from Schedule G, line 1a (minus any foreign tax credit from Schedule G, line 2a).	38	
39	**Alternative minimum tax.** Subtract line 38 from line 37. If zero or less, enter -0-. Enter here and on Schedule G, line 6	39	

Part IV—Line 35 Computation Using Maximum Capital Gains Rates

Caution: *If the estate or trust did not complete Part V of Schedule D (Form 1041), complete lines 19 through 26 of Schedule D (as refigured for the AMT, if necessary) before completing this part.*

40	Enter the amount from line 34	40	
41	Enter the amount from Schedule D (Form 1041), line 26 (as refigured for AMT, if necessary)	41	
42	Enter the amount from Schedule D (Form 1041), line 24 (as refigured for AMT, if necessary)	42	
43	Add lines 41 and 42. If zero or less, enter -0-	43	
44	Enter the amount from Schedule D (Form 1041), line 21 (as refigured for AMT, if necessary)	44	
45	Enter the **smaller** of line 43 or line 44	45	
46	Subtract line 45 from line 40. If zero or less, enter -0-	46	
47	If line 46 is $175,000 or less, multiply line 46 by 26% (.26). Otherwise, multiply line 46 by 28% (.28) and subtract $3,500 from the result . . . . ▶	47	
48	Enter the amount from Schedule D (Form 1041), line 35 (as figured for the regular tax) . . .	48	
49	Enter the **smallest** of line 40, line 41, or line 48	49	
50	Multiply line 49 by 10% (.10) . . . . ▶	50	
51	Enter the **smaller** of line 40 or line 41	51	
52	Enter the amount from line 49	52	
53	Subtract line 52 from line 51. If zero or less, enter -0-	53	
54	Multiply line 53 by 20% (.20) . . . . ▶	54	
55	Enter the amount from line 40	55	
56	Add lines 46, 49, and 53	56	
57	Subtract line 56 from line 55	57	
58	Multiply line 57 by 25% (.25) . . . . ▶	58	
59	Add lines 47, 50, 54, and 58	59	
60	If line 40 is $175,000 or less, multiply line 40 by 26% (.26). Otherwise, multiply line 40 by 28% (.28) and subtract $3,500 from the result	60	
61	Enter the **smaller** of line 59 or line 60 here and on line 35 . . . . ▶	61	

243

SCHEDULE D

SCHEDULE D (Form 1041) Department of the Treasury Internal Revenue Service	Capital Gains and Losses ▶ Attach to Form 1041 (or Form 5227). See the separate instructions for Form 1041 (or Form 5227).	OMB No. 1545-0092 1998
Name of estate or trust		Employer identification number

Note: *Form 5227 filers need to complete ONLY Parts I and II.*

Part I Short-Term Capital Gains and Losses—Assets Held One Year or Less

(a) Description of property (Example, 100 shares 7% preferred of "Z" Co.)	(b) Date acquired (mo., day, yr.)	(c) Date sold (mo., day, yr.)	(d) Sales price	(e) Cost or other basis (see page 26)	(f) GAIN or (LOSS) (col. (d) less col. (e))	
1						

2 Short-term capital gain or (loss) from Forms 4684, 6252, 6781, and 8824 . .	2	
3 Net short-term gain or (loss) from partnerships, S corporations, and other estates or trusts	3	
4 Short-term capital loss carryover. Enter the amount, if any, from line 9 of the 1997 Capital Loss Carryover Worksheet	4 (	)
5 **Net short-term gain or (loss).** Combine lines 1 through 4 in column (f). Enter here and on line 14 below . . . . ▶	5	

Part II Long-Term Capital Gains and Losses—Assets Held More Than One Year

(a) Description of property (Example, 100 shares 7% preferred of "Z" Co.)	(b) Date acquired (mo., day, yr.)	(c) Date sold (mo., day, yr.)	(d) Sales price	(e) Cost or other basis (see page 26)	(f) GAIN or (LOSS) (col. (d) less col. (e))	(g) 28% RATE GAIN or (LOSS) *(see instr. below)
6						

7 Long-term capital gain or (loss) from Forms 2439, 4684, 6252, 6781, and 8824. .	7	
8 Net long-term gain or (loss) from partnerships, S corporations, and other estates or trusts .	8	
9 Capital gain distributions	9	
10 Gain from Form 4797, Part I	10	
11 Long-term capital loss carryover. Enter in both columns (f) and (g) the amount, if any, from line 14, of the 1997 Capital Loss Carryover Worksheet	11 ( )( )
12 Combine lines 6 through 11 in column (g)	12	
13 **Net long-term gain or (loss).** Combine lines 6 through 11 in column (f). Enter here and on line 15 below . . . . ▶	13	

***28% Rate Gain or (Loss)** includes **all** "collectibles gains and losses" (as defined on page 27 of the instructions) and up to 50% of the eligible gain on qualified small business stock (see page 25 of the instructions).

Part III Summary of Parts I and II

		(1) Beneficiaries' (see page 27)	(2) Estate's or trust's	(3) Total
14 **Net short-term gain or (loss)** (from line 5 above) . . .	14			
15 **Net long-term gain or (loss):**				
a 28% rate gain or (loss) (from line 12 above)	15a			
b Unrecaptured section 1250 gain (see worksheet on page 26)	15b			
c Total for year (from line 13 above).	15c			
16 **Total net gain or (loss).** Combine lines 14 and 15c . ▶	16			

Note: *If line 16, column (3), is a net gain, enter the gain on Form 1041, line 4. If lines 15c and 16, column (2) are net gains, go to Part V, and DO NOT complete Part IV. If line 16, column (3), is a net loss, complete Part IV and the **Capital Loss Carryover Worksheet**, as necessary.*

For Paperwork Reduction Act Notice, see the Instructions for Form 1041.   Cat. No. 11376V   Schedule D (Form 1041) 1998

SCHEDULE D – page 2

Schedule D (Form 1041) 1998   Page **2**

Part IV   Capital Loss Limitation

17 Enter here and enter as a (loss) on Form 1041, line 4, the **smaller** of:
  a The loss on line 16, column (3); **or**
  b $3,000 . . . . **17** (   )
*If the loss on line 16, column (3) is more than $3,000, OR if Form 1041, page 1, line 22, is a loss, complete the **Capital Loss Carryover Worksheet** on page 27 of the instructions to determine your capital loss carryover.*

Part V   **Tax Computation Using Maximum Capital Gains Rates** (Complete this part **only** if both lines 15c and 16 in column (2) are gains, and Form 1041, line 22 is more than zero.)

18 Enter taxable income from Form 1041, line 22.	**18**
19 Enter the **smaller** of line 15c or 16 in column (2). **19**	
20 If you are filing Form 4952, enter the amount from Form 4952, line 4e . **20**	
21 Subtract line 20 from line 19. If zero or less, enter -0- **21**	
22 Combine lines 14 and 15a, column (2). If zero or less, enter -0- . . . **22**	
23 Enter the **smaller** of line 15a, column (2), or line 22, but not less than zero **23**	
24 Enter the amount from line 15b, column (2). **24**	
25 Add lines 23 and 24 . . . . **25**	
26 Subtract line 25 from line 21. If zero or less, enter -0-	**26**
27 Subtract line 26 from line 18. If zero or less, enter -0-	**27**
28 Enter the **smaller** of line 18 or $1,700	**28**
29 Enter the **smaller** of line 27 or line 28	**29**
30 Subtract line 21 from line 18. If zero or less, enter -0-	**30**
31 Enter the **larger** of line 29 or line 30	**31**
32 Tax on amount on line 31 from the 1998 Tax Rate Schedule . . . . ▶	**32**
33 Enter the amount from line 28	**33**
34 Enter the amount from line 27	**34**
35 Subtract line 34 from line 33. If zero or less, enter -0-	**35**
36 Multiply line 35 by 10% (.10) . . . . ▶	**36**
37 Enter the **smaller** of line 18 or line 26	**37**
38 Enter the amount from line 35	**38**
39 Subtract line 38 from line 37. If zero or less, enter -0-	**39**
40 Multiply line 39 by 20% (.20) . . . . ▶	**40**
41 Enter the **smaller** of line 21 or line 24	**41**
42 Add lines 21 and 31 . . . . **42**	
43 Enter the amount from line 18 . . . . **43**	
44 Subtract line 43 from line 42. If zero or less, enter -0-	**44**
45 Subtract line 44 from line 41. If zero or less, enter -0-	**45**
46 Multiply line 45 by 25% (.25) . . . . ▶	**46**
47 Enter the amount from line 18	**47**
48 Add lines 31, 35, 39, and 45	**48**
49 Subtract line 48 from line 47	**49**
50 Multiply line 49 by 28% (.28) . . . . ▶	**50**
51 Add lines 32, 36, 40, 46, and 50	**51**
52 Tax on the amount on line 18 from the 1998 Tax Rate Schedule	**52**
53 **Tax on taxable income (including capital gains).** Enter the **smaller** of line 51 or line 52 here and on line 1a of Schedule G, Form 1041. . . . . ▶	**53**

245

SCHEDULE K-1

SCHEDULE K-1 (Form 1041)	Beneficiary's Share of Income, Deductions, Credits, etc.	OMB No. 1545-0092
Department of the Treasury / Internal Revenue Service	for the calendar year 1998, or fiscal year beginning .... , 1998, ending .... , 19 .... ▶ Complete a separate Schedule K-1 for each beneficiary.	1998

Name of trust or decedent's estate

☐ Amended K-1
☐ Final K-1

Beneficiary's identifying number ▶	Estate's or trust's EIN ▶
Beneficiary's name, address, and ZIP code	Fiduciary's name, address, and ZIP code

(a) Allocable share item		(b) Amount	(c) Calendar year 1998 Form 1040 filers enter the amounts in column (b) on:
1	Interest.	1	Schedule B, Part I, line 1
2	Ordinary dividends .	2	Schedule B, Part II, line 5
3	Net short-term capital gain .	3	Schedule D, line 5
4	Net long-term capital gain: **a** 28% rate gain . .	4a	Schedule D, line 12, column (g)
b	Unrecaptured section 1250 gain	4b	Line 11 of the worksheet for Schedule D, line 25
c	Total for year.	4c	Schedule D, line 12, column (f)
5a	Annuities, royalties, and other nonpassive income before directly apportioned deductions	5a	Schedule E, Part III, column (f)
b	Depreciation	5b	} Include on the applicable line of the appropriate tax form
c	Depletion	5c	
d	Amortization	5d	
6a	Trade or business, rental real estate, and other rental income before directly apportioned deductions (see instructions) .	6a	Schedule E, Part III
b	Depreciation	6b	} Include on the applicable line of the appropriate tax form
c	Depletion	6c	
d	Amortization	6d	
7	Income for minimum tax purposes	7	
8	Income for regular tax purposes (add lines 1, 2, 3, 4c, 5a, and 6a)	8	
9	Adjustment for minimum tax purposes (subtract line 8 from line 7).	9	Form 6251, line 12
10	Estate tax deduction (including certain generation-skipping transfer taxes)	10	Schedule A, line 27
11	Foreign taxes.	11	Form 1116 or Schedule A (Form 1040), line 8
12	Adjustments and tax preference items (itemize):		
a	Accelerated depreciation	12a	} Include on the applicable line of Form 6251
b	Depletion	12b	
c	Amortization	12c	
d	Exclusion items	12d	1999 Form 8801
13	Deductions in the final year of trust or decedent's estate:		
a	Excess deductions on termination (see instructions)	13a	Schedule A, line 22
b	Short-term capital loss carryover	13b	Schedule D, line 5
c	Long-term capital loss carryover	13c ( )	Schedule D, line 12, columns (f) and (g)
d	Net operating loss (NOL) carryover for regular tax purposes	13d ( )	Form 1040, line 21
e	NOL carryover for minimum tax purposes	13e	See the instructions for Form 6251, line 20
f	....	13f	} Include on the applicable line of the appropriate tax form
g	....	13g	
14	Other (itemize):		
a	Payments of estimated taxes credited to you . .	14a	Form 1040, line 58
b	Tax-exempt interest	14b	Form 1040, line 8b
c	....	14c	} Include on the applicable line of the appropriate tax form
d	....	14d	
e	....	14e	
f	....	14f	
g	....	14g	
h	....	14h	

For Paperwork Reduction Act Notice, see the Instructions for Form 1041.   Cat. No. 11380D   Schedule K-1 (Form 1041) 1998

FORM 1310

Form **1310** (Rev. March 1995) Department of the Treasury Internal Revenue Service	**Statement of Person Claiming Refund Due a Deceased Taxpayer** ▶ See instructions below and on back.	OMB No. 1545-0073 Attachment Sequence No. **87**

Tax year decedent was due a refund:

| Calendar year _____, or other tax year beginning _____ , 19 ___ , and ending _____ , 19 ___ |

Please type or print	Name of decedent	Date of death	Decedent's social security number
	Name of person claiming refund		
	Home address (number and street). If you have a P.O. box, see instructions.		Apt. no.
	City, town or post office, state, and ZIP code. If you have a foreign address, see instructions.		

Part I Check the box that applies to you. Check only one box. **Be sure to complete Part III below.**

A ☐ Surviving spouse requesting reissuance of a refund check. See instructions.

B ☐ Court-appointed or certified personal representative. You may have to attach a court certificate showing your appointment. See instructions.

C ☐ Person, **other** than A or B, claiming refund for the decedent's estate. Also, complete Part II. You may have to attach a copy of the proof of death. See instructions.

Part II Complete this part only if you checked the box on line C above.

		Yes	No
1	Did the decedent leave a will?		
2a	Has a court appointed a personal representative for the estate of the decedent?		
b	If you answered "No" to 2a, will one be appointed?		
	If you answered "Yes" to 2a or 2b, the personal representative must file for the refund.		
3	As the person claiming the refund for the decedent's estate, will you pay out the refund according to the laws of the state where the decedent was a legal resident?		
	If you answered "No" to 3, a refund cannot be made until you submit a court certificate showing your appointment as personal representative or other evidence that you are entitled under state law to receive the refund.		

Part III Signature and verification. All filers must complete this part.

I request a refund of taxes overpaid by or on behalf of the decedent. Under penalties of perjury, I declare that I have examined this claim, and to the best of my knowledge and belief, it is true, correct, and complete.

Signature of person claiming refund ▶ _____   Date ▶ _____

247

Index

■ ■ ■ ■ ■ ■ ■

FREE Subscription Offer!

FINANCIAL FOCUS

Wealth Producer and Protector

February 1999

Produced by

Jack W. Everett, CFP, AIMC

Volume XIX

Issue VIII

Dear Clients & Friends:

Last month I said that I expected the stock market to be full of ups and downs in 1999. It sure has started off that way. Within the first two weeks the Dow Jones Industrial Average went up about 5%, started dropping, had a 200 plus drop in one day, followed by an almost identical 200 point plus gain the next day. You can expect to see these roller coaster thrills all year, just don't let them worry you so much that you pull out of the market.

Watching the STOCK MARKET EVERY DAY COULD BE HAZARDOUS TO YOUR HEALTH & WEALTH

One of the New Year's resolutions that I recommended for you in the January issue of Financial Focus was that you should not watch the stock market every day. The reason that I recommended this is because watching the market swings over short time periods is known to cause ulcers, heart attacks, high blood pressure and dumb investment decisions. **Short term fluctuations are worrisome, but most often meaningless. It's the long term results that count.**

I thought more about this last month when one of my clients contacted me with concerns about an investment that he had for the past seven months. Although the investment had made a 10% return for the period, it had lost value for two of the months and for four of the months had earned less than money market returns. If it hadn't been for one month with a large return, it would not have made money for the seven month period.

This is exactly how the stock market works. **When you**

invest in the stock market through individual stocks, mutual funds, variable annuities or money managers; you will not be receiving interest. Your account will not grow at a steady rate. The value of your account will vary depending upon two factors. The first factor is dividends paid to you by the companies in your portfolio. These dividends are not guaranteed, but paid out of profits as determined by the Board of Directors of each company. The second factor is the current market price for the shares of stock, as determined by what investors are willing to pay for these shares.

The price of the shares of stock of each company is subject to whims of the investors. **They may use many sophisticated techniques to determine at what price they are willing to buy or sell a stock, but the actual price is often determined by the emotions of fear and greed. The result is that, short term, the stock markets are very inefficient and somewhat unstable. Over the long run, they reflect the value of the**

2140 Professional Drive, Suite 105 — Roseville, CA 95661-3734

(916) 791-1447 – (800) 678-3872 – Fax (916) 791-3444 – e-mail jeverett@quiknet.com

Special offer to readers of
The Truth about Trusts

Enjoy a FREE three-month trial subscription to Jack Everett's highly aclaimed newsletter, *Financial Focus: Wealth Producer and Protector,* a $10 value.

Keep informed about your investments, trusts, and taxes with this timely and lively monthly newsletter. Jack Canfield, co-author of the Chicken Soup books, says, "I look forward to receiving your newsletter each month."

■ ■

Yes, please send my free 3-month trial subscription to *Financial Focus.* I understand I am under no obligation due to this request.

Name _____

Address _____

City _____ State _____ Zip _____

Mail this form to:

Financial Focus   or:
c/o Financial & Tax Planning Center   *fax:* (916) 791-3444
2140 Professional Drive, Suite 105   *phone:* (800) 678-3872
Roseville, CA 95661   *e-mail:* jeverett@quiknet.com